HOW TO FIX CYBER BULLYING

TESKO

Assessing The Crisis of School Interventions

Ben Wood Johnson

HOW TO FIX
CYBERBULLYING

TESKO

Ben Wood Johnson

TESKO PUBLISHING PRESS

Middletown, PA

Johnson, Wood Ben, 1975—
　　　How to Fix Cyberbullying / Ben Wood
　　　Johnson.
　　　p. cm.
Includes bibliographical references and index.

ISBN-13: 978-1-948600-38-5 (pbk: permanent paper)
ISBN-10: 1-948600-38-2
　　　1. Education, urban/rural—United States.
　　　2. School policy—United States. 3. School
　　　intervention programs—United States.

The information illustrated in this book was compiled for a school project. The analysis is based on class notes and other materials.

Tesko Publishing

TESKO

Cover Illustration Wood Oliver

For Charlemagne

ACKNOWLEDGMENTS

I WANT TO THANK THE PERSONS who contributed to this work since its original conception. The materials that culminated in this book include class notes and other works, which had been collected and completed while I was a graduate student at Penn State University. Over the course of my education in the Educational Leadership Program at Penn State, I completed several essays and academic papers, which, in one form or another, are a part of the present publication.

Publisher's Acknowledgments: Several people contributed to this work. Their feedback, comments, and recommendations helped me refurbish the present edition. The individuals who contributed to this new edition include Wolden Olivier (for his contributions during formatting and content cleaning), Xaon Wood (for his contributions during manuscript revisions and formatting review), and Danny Chan (for his contributions in content formatting and content editing). Thank you all.

CONTENTS

Acknowledgments   *vii*

Preface   *xi*

Introduction   *1*

PART ONE: UNDERSTANDING CYBERBULLYING

1. A New Social Problem   7

2. Bullying and Elementary Education   15

3. A Lack of Clear Definitions   21

4. The Nature of Cyberbullying   27

5. Student Misbehaving Online   33

PART TWO: THE NEED FOR SCHOOL ACTIONS

6. Reporting Online Conduct   41

7. The Need to Eradicate Bullying   47

8. School Interventions and Existing Policies   53

9. An Initiative-taking Approach   59

PART THREE: POLICIES ABOUT CYBERBULLYING

10. Defying Popular Viewpoints   65

11. The Extent of the Intervention Crisis   69

12. Deficiency of Policy Guidelines   75

13. A Broad Policy Approach   79

PART FOUR: THE REALITIES OF SCHOOL POLICIES

14. Popular Assumptions About School Policies   85

15. Misguided Policies   89

16. Gaps in the Literature   93

PART FIVE: EXAMINING COURT DECISIONS

17. Understanding the Role of the Courts   101

18. Legal Implications   105

19. The Courts and Cyberbullying   109

20. Assessing a Recent Study   115

    Afterword   119

    References   123

    Index   137

    About the author   143

    Also by   145

PREFACE

ONLINE BULLYING IS NOT a mystery. There is no dearth of information about the phenomenon. The literature is saturated with works that elaborate on the problem and its effects on society. Notwithstanding, the present work is much more surgical. The focus here is on school interventions.

While most observers believe that schools cannot intervene in online incidents, there is also the view that the reality of school policy on this issue is more complex than most people would admit. The argument could be made that there is enough evidence to suggest that schools can (and do) intervene when students misbehave on the Internet. But a noteworthy probability, which might hamper school interventions is the deficiency of clear policy guidance. Hence, it is important to grasp the crux of the debate.

The present work canvases the literature. It offers notable

observations about the topic. This short compilation outlines a thorough, but to the point, analysis of both the legal and the administrative hurdles that often characterize school interventions in bullying, particularly online bullying.

This edition is not broad in scope. But it discusses the nature of the school policies, which had been designed expressly to guide school interventions in similar incidents. The book provides valuable information about the current conversation. Also, the text relates the potential reason interventions might be antagonistic. It discusses the degree to which students misbehave online.

While the literature is laden with works that posit that most school professionals are operating in the dark when intervening in online bullying, the likelihood, albeit back by previous research, points to the possibility that most school districts do not have the right policies in place to deal with the problem. The present analysis denies the idea that there is an intervention crisis in cyberbullying.

This edition discusses arguments that are often echoed in the literature. It examines the views that scholars and school professionals often denote to relate the seriousness of online bullying. It explores the predicament that school officials often face when they intervene in similar incidents.

The text sheds some lights on the debate. The argument echoed throughout these pages is that misconceptions drive the debate about school interventions. The book challenges the idea that the courts are the sole culprits in schools' inability to address online incidents.

A scarcity of policy guidelines might cause the made-out school interventions crisis. That deficiency might be at the roots of legal disputes. The book highlights drawbacks in the literature. It explains how the courts have shaped cyberbullying laws over the last few years.

This compilation is not in-depth, considering the extent of the conversation about the subject. The book was not designed to be copious. It is an extract from a series of articles, which I compiled years ago. Despite the outlined concessions, the goal of this analysis—at least in the present context—is to provide valuable insights about the extent of online bullying. It is important to differentiate between facts and myths about the issues.

Although the book does not explain the bullying phenomenon in all its intricacies, it offers a notable assessment of the contentions that plague the current discourse. Therefore, the information gleaned from this work might help you discover the essentiality of the bullying crisis. The book might help you understand the need for sound policies to guide school interventions.

You may learn more about online bullying by reviewing other books, which are more thorough on the subject. The Internet is filled with literary and audiovisual resources, including books, articles, blog post, and videos, which might help you learn more about cyberbullying. A noteworthy website is the Cyberbullying Research Center *(https://cyberbullying.org)* spearheaded by Dr. Justin W. Patchin and Dr. Sameer Hinduja.

As an expert in the field, I have also compiled a few materials on the subject. Some of them are listed toward the end of the manuscript. You might find them informative.

For now, I strongly encourage you to immerse yourself in this literary primer. The present analysis centers on the fundamentals of online bullying. It explores the nature of school response to the problem. Join me in this intellectual journey.

Good reading!
Ben Wood Johnson, Ph.D.
Fall 2022

INTRODUCTION

CYBERBULLYING IS A REAL PROBLEM around the world. It is all thanks to the Internet, which is the work of an array of pioneering scientists, programmers, and engineers.[1] As one of the most effective pieces of technologies in the world,[2] the Internet could be understood as a network of networks, which purpose is to facilitate interconnection among networks. [3] Over the years, the phenomenon known as bullying has morphed into different

---

[1] Evan Andrews, "Who Invented the Internet? - Ask History," HISTORY.com, December 18, 2013, http://www.history.com/news/ask-history/who-invented-the-internet.

[2] Ranjan Mahato, "History of the Internet and Popularity of the Internet.," HubPages, May 22, 2013, http://hubpages.com/technology/History-of-the-Internet-and-specialty-of-the-Internet.

[3] Leslie Daigle, "On the Nature of the Internet," Paper series, Global Commission on Internet Governance (The Centre for International Governance Innovation and Chatham House, March 16, 2015), 4, https://www.cigionline.org/sites/default/files/gcig_paper_no7.pdf.

practices and has taken many iterations. But its effects are still palpable in social settings driven by an insatiable need for egocentrism and the rampant reliance on technology to express moments of allegory and moments of frustrations.

The title of this book says it all. It seeks to help you, regardless of your profession or area of interest, deal with cyberbullying. Even if you are not a school administrator, a parent, or a student, you might learn something valuable from this work. The text discusses strategies, which might help school professionals address cyber-related incidents.

Admittedly, this edition is an ambitious project. Could this book really help fix online bullying? I will let you be the judge of that. But I recommend that you do so based on your assessment of the views outlined throughout these pages. Regardless of your assessment of this work, it may help you understand the nature of harassment on the Internet, which, according to the US Equal Employment Opportunity Commission (2016), is understood as "unwelcome conduct that is based on race, color, religion, sex (including sexual orientation, gender identity, or pregnancy), national origin, older age (beginning at age 40), disability, or genetic information (including family medical history)." Harassment is offensive in nature and generally involves "offensive jokes, slurs, epithets or name calling, physical assaults or threats, intimidation, ridicule or mockery, insults or put-downs, offensive objects or pictures."[4]

---

[4] U.S. Equal Employment Opportunity Commission, "Harassment," 2016, http://www.eeoc.gov/laws/types/harassment.cfm.

The reality of online bullying can be different in the real world, since there is no consensus in the current conversation about what makes up this occurrence. Misunderstanding the concept of bullying can lead to inconsistent approaches to solving the problems bred by this phenomenon. The present analysis is unique; it offers the reader an overview of the existing literature on school interventions. The book explores the particularities of existing discussions vis-à-vis the extent of school policies designed specifically to address cyberbullying incidents, whether they occurred on school grounds or elsewhere.

This work, brief though it is, explores the intricacies of student conduct online. The concept of cyberbullying has abruptly entered the academic lexicon, if not the public consciousness, over the past few years. Remember, the text is primarily exploratory, as it does not relate the minutiae of the problem. But below, I summarize the current discourse debating the degree to which schools have the right policies in place to address electronic misdeeds by K-12 students on the Internet.

As we move along in our analysis, a few issues are worthy of note. For example, the book does not discuss every incident related to online bullying; at least, it does not do so in great length in the present context. The text does not examine the nature of every online misconduct; it does not relate the traits of commonly known cases and their place of occurrence. The book does not elaborate on the prevalence of online bullying in American schools.

Despite the noted limits, the book is to the point. Its arguments are intuitive; they are succinct; they are informative. Plus, the book clarifies the current cyber harassment predicament, which afflicts many societies, though our analysis centers on the United States. Let us explore the online singularity further. Let us make sense of this new social trend.

PART ONE: UNDERSTANDING CYBERBULLYING

Keywords: School officials, harsh punishments, school interventions, online incidents, disciplinary reach, legal actions, and cyber-criminality.

1

A New Social Problem

Bullying, at least in its raw form, is not a novel social quandary. Although it is more prevalent in the workplace, with 30% of adult Americans report being bulging at work and 66% reported being aware of bullying at work, [1] the phenomenon is more prevalent than most people realize. In one way or another, bullying has been a part of the social experience. But this conduct is

---

[1] Gary Namie, "2021 WBI U.S. Workplace Bullying Survey," *Workplace Bullying Institute* (blog), February 24, 2021, https://workplacebullying.org/2021-wbi-survey/; Gary Namie and Ruth Namie, "Are You Being Bullied At Work?," *Workplace Bullying Institute* (blog), 2022, https://workplacebullying.org/.

persistent; it is insidious, notably in most school settings.[2]

While cyberbullying is a recent occurrence, [3] facets of behaviors, which could be discerned as online bullying, are not part of a novel experience. Just like its traditional counterpart, online harassment, or facets of this occurrence, has been around for a long time. The law has always proactive on this issue. In fact, the first known iteration of online aggressions, which resulted with a conviction, could be traced back to 2008.

Lori Drew, a Missouri mother, was on trial in a landmark cyberbullying case.[4] She created a phony account on MySpace, impersonating a teenage boy (Josh Evans), which was seemingly designed to trick a teenager,[5] Megan Meier, who was 13 years old at the time. Megan later committed suicide.

Drew was found guilty of a lesser charge.[6] But she was tried for more significant charges, including a fourth count of conspiracy against Megan, which would have resulted in a felony conviction, Drew was convicted of three misdemeanor computer fraud

---

[2] Susan Maree Ryan, "The Internet Playground: One School's Experience of Cyberbullying," 2017.

[3] Pam Nilan et al., "Youth, Social Media, and Cyberbullying Among Australian Youth: 'Sick Friends,'" *Social Media + Society* 1, no. 2 (July 1, 2015): 2056305115604848, https://doi.org/10.1177/2056305115604848.

[4] Jennifer Steinhauer, "Verdict in MySpace Suicide Case," *The New York Times*, November 26, 2008, sec. U.S., https://www.nytimes.com/2008/11/27/us/27myspace.html.

[5] Ibid.

[6] CBS News, "Cyberbully Mom Guilty Of Lesser Charge," November 26, 2008, https://www.cbsnews.com/news/cyberbully-mom-guilty-of-lesser-charge/.

charges.[7]

Although Lori Drew was the first known legal case involving cyberbullying, it was not the last. In 2014, for example, a jury found Robert Bishop, an 18-year-old from North Carolina, guilty of cyberbullying under the state statute.[8] Bishop used Facebook to harass and intimidate a boy, which led to his arrest. These two cases are among the most publicized. But countless others have faced legal consequences for their online misconduct.

***

Experiencing harassment on the Internet is a real occurrence. Most people have experienced cyberbullying in one form or another. Online bullying is obtrusive; it is invasive. Dealing with this calamity can be depressing, considering its demoralizing nature. Most people use the Internet as a means to express themselves. Some people use this tool as a way to oppress or even to suppress others.

For most people, bullying, whether it results from a face-to-face confrontation or from a sour cyberspace interaction, feels like an invasion of one's privacy. Thus, cyberbullying could be understood as the curse of technologically subservient societies, which is on par with the notion that technologies may make up a major challenge

---

[7] Steinhauer, "Verdict in MySpace Suicide Case."

[8] Faith S. Abubey, "County Convicts First Suspect Under Cyber Bullying Law," wfmynews2.com, February 6, 2014, https://www.wfmynews2.com/article/news/local/county-convicts-first-suspect-under-cyber-bullying-law/83-313777058.

for populations across the world. [9]   But the implications of experiencing any form of harassment or any other types of intimidations (be it in-person or online) can have irreversible consequences on the victim. It is best to avoid such an ordeal.

Within the last few years, bullying acts have become rampant in society. Technological advances made the situation even worse. Likewise, responding to online bullying come with fracas. It is a major problem facing most American educators. This predicament is not just a school reality; it is also a societal crisis.

Online bullying, observers are convinced, is more pervasive than a face-to-face (traditional) bullying conduct. Although the causes and effects of online bullying are unsettled in the literature, [10] because of recent advances in Internet technologies, there is a new form of bullying, which is wreaking havoc in most societies. In the most simplistic terms, this happening is known as online bullying.

Online bullying poses a threat to the social and emotional development of adolescents. [11]   In recent years, the phenomenon has been labeled as a new form of bullying or online harassment. [12]

---

[9] Jeremy Hsu, "Can Humans Survive?," LiveScience.com, March 7, 2022, http://www.livescience.com/9956-humans-survive.html.

[10] Justin W Patchin and Sameer Hinduja, "Bullies Move beyond the Schoolyard: A Preliminary Look at Cyberbullying," *Youth Violence and Juvenile Justice* 4, no. 2 (2006): 148–69.

[11] Juliana Raskauskas and Ann D Stoltz, "Involvement in Traditional and Electronic Bullying among Adolescents.," *Developmental Psychology* 43, no. 3 (2007): 564.

[12] Ibid.; Robert Slonje and Peter K Smith, "Cyberbullying: Another Main Type of Bullying?," *Scandinavian Journal of Psychology* 49, no. 2 (2008): 147–54.

This occurrence is a permutation of face-to-face harassment. [13] Considering the similitude of this type of harassment with the more common bullying in schoolyards, the phenomenon is described as a "new bottle but old wine." [14] Most observers consider this appellation an accurate assessment of an important problem in society, which is creating incommensurable damages and interpersonal problems.

A much-popular nomenclature to delineate this type of online misconduct among individuals is cyberbullying. Other terminologies include the terms electronic bullying and online social cruelty.[15] Cyberbullying is often described as harassment through the Internet and through other electronic gadgets, including mobile phones.[16] This form of bullying has added to the potential damage the Internet can cause for and to young people.[17] Cyberbullying is affecting millions of students.[18]

As the name suggests, online bullying occurs on the Internet.

---

[13] Patchin and Hinduja, "Bullies Move beyond the Schoolyard: A Preliminary Look at Cyberbullying."

[14] Qing Li, "New Bottle but Old Wine: A Research of Cyberbullying in Schools," *Computers in Human Behavior* 23, no. 4 (2007): 1777–91.

[15] Robin M Kowalski and Susan P Limber, "Electronic Bullying among Middle School Students," *Journal of Adolescent Health* 41, no. 6 (2007): S22–30.

[16] Peter K Smith et al., "Cyberbullying: Its Nature and Impact in Secondary School Pupils," *Journal of Child Psychology and Psychiatry* 49, no. 4 (2008): 376–85.

[17] Ryan, "The Internet Playground: One School's Experience of Cyberbullying."

[18] Jaana Juvonen and Elisheva F Gross, "Extending the School Grounds?—Bullying Experiences in Cyberspace," *Journal of School Health* 78, no. 9 (2008): 496–505.

Almost half of bullies use a similar medium (that is, the Internet) to harass others.[19] They use this medium to send lewd images of themselves to others. Sexting, for example, is a major form of online harassment, which studies found to be prevalent among older youth, though females are likely to receive sexts massages at a higher rate than males do.[20] But two separate studies (2010 and 2016) found that several middle school and high school students admitted to sending naked or semi-naked images of themselves to others.[21]

With sending and receiving text messages, approximately 14% of middle school and high school students have sent explicit images to others.[22] About 23% of them have received similar images from others.[23] But it would be misguided to classify this occurrence as a onetime event. Bullying, be it in the cyberspace or elsewhere, must be a recurrent behavior.

Most bullying cases involved a conduct that occurred over three

---

[19] Qing Li, "Cyberbullying in Schools: A Research of Gender Differences," *School Psychology International* 27, no. 2 (2006): 157–70.

[20] Camille Mori et al., "Are Youth Sexting Rates Still on the Rise? A Meta-Analytic Update," *The Journal of Adolescent Health: Official Publication of the Society for Adolescent Medicine* 70, no. 4 (April 2022): 531–39, https://doi.org/10.1016/j.jadohealth.2021.10.026.

[21] Sameer Hinduja and Justin W. Patchin, "Teen Sexting – A Brief Guide for Educators and Parents," Cyberbullying Research Center, 2022, https://cyberbullying.org/sexting-research-summary-2022.pdf.

[22] Justin W. Patchin, "The Status of Sexting Laws Across the United States," *Cyberbullying Research Center* (blog), August 18, 2022, https://cyberbullying.org/the-status-of-sexting-laws-across-the-united-states.

[23] Ibid.

times in a row.[24] Thus, an online bullying incident, depending on the many forms it might take, is a persistent social problem, which most modern societies have found difficult, if not impossible to eradicate, even to address properly. The problem of bullying is more pervasive in school settings than it might be in other places.

---

[24] Li, "Cyberbullying in Schools: A Research of Gender Differences."

2

BULLYING AND ELEMENTARY EDUCATION

In education, online bullying is more common than most people realize. [1] This category of harassment is prevalent among school-age children and young adults. However, online bullying, to restate, is a major problem in most societies. It is undeniable that the Internet is a dangerous place for children and adolescents. [2]

---

[1] Patchin and Hinduja, "Bullies Move beyond the Schoolyard: A Preliminary Look at Cyberbullying."

[2] Robert S Tokunaga, "Following You Home from School: A Critical Review and Synthesis of Research on Cyberbullying Victimization," *Computers in Human Behavior* 26, no. 3 (2010): 277–87.

Children are exposed to negative content online.[3] Such exposure often affects the family.[4]

Despite the popularity of online bullying among school-age children, this occurrence is even much more prevalent among lower secondary schools.[5] Younger children are more prone to become victimize by cyberbullies. Most observers believe that cyberbullying is causing so much damage in K-12 educational settings that it should not be overlooked. Thus, the phenomenon cannot go unaddressed, though most youth report positive experiences on the Internet.[6]

It would be inconsiderate to aggregate the online bullying reality as solely a school problem. Because of the prevalence of Internet technologies, online bullying is not only limited to public schools.[7] Considering the mobile nature of Internet-related technologies, Internet users, namely young people, can be vulnerable anywhere; they are susceptible to online bullies in the cyberspace.

Another consideration is that the Internet can be unavoidable

---

3 Chang-Hoan Cho and Hongsik John Cheon, "Children's Exposure to Negative Internet Content: Effects of Family Context," *Journal of Broadcasting & Electronic Media* 49, no. 4 (December 1, 2005): 488–509, https://doi.org/10.1207/s15506878jobem4904_8.

4 Ibid.

5 Slonje and Smith, "Cyberbullying: Another Main Type of Bullying?"

6 Michele L Ybarra and Kimberly J Mitchell, "Online Aggressor/Targets, Aggressors, and Targets: A Comparison of Associated Youth Characteristics," *Journal of Child Psychology and Psychiatry* 45, no. 7 (2004): 1308–16.

7 Juvonen and Gross, "Extending the School Grounds?—Bullying Experiences in Cyberspace."

for most people. In 2010 alone, it was determined that over 97% of American youth had a presence on the Internet.[8] Put differently, the problem posed by this medium more than a decade ago remains a critical concern in today's society, which parents and school officials continue to juggle with, to no avail, some might say. In twelve years, the problem has only worsened.

The previous assertion may seem far-fetched to most observers. However, there is enough data out there to corroborate that contention. For example, a 2010 report noted that about 20–40% of youth have experienced cyberbullying at least once in their lifetime.[9] The situation has not changed, though it is even more complex nowadays.

As of 2022, the Internet is more popular than it was before. About 69.0% of the world's population uses the Internet in one form or another.[10] This tool is now described as a media; else, it is a medium where people gather to share information or to get information. The Internet is also used as an entertainment medium. The popularity of Internet-related devices is an irrefutable reality, which few could grapple with in today's society. Most people have an Internet presence, which may be outside the realm of their will or their personal desires, considering that many view this medium

---

[8] Tokunaga, "Following You Home from School: A Critical Review and Synthesis of Research on Cyberbullying Victimization."

[9] Ibid.

[10] Internet World Stats, "Internet Growth Statistics: Today's Road to e-Commerce and Global Trade Internet Technology Reports," July 31, 2022, http://www.internetworldstats.com/emarketing.htm.

as a utility means rules, which can be enforced.[11] But every aspect of today's life involves an Internet presence.

Although the internet has both positive and negative effects, it has not boded well for children and young adolescents, though in 2009, young adolescents were considered the primary users of the Internet.[12] Just as a decade ago, cyberbullying remains prevalent in many school districts across the United States. School officials struggle to contain online bullying incidents, which often occur on a peer-to-peer basis. The situation is even more precarious for young students. The Internet is a source of digital distress for young adolescents.[13] In induces stressors, such as mean and harassing personal attacks, public shaming and humiliation, impersonation, feeling smothered, pressure to comply with requests for access, and breaking and entering into digital accounts and devices.[14] This reality poses a major challenge for young adolescents, as they do not always have the means to cope with the stress associated with living in the digital world.[15]

---

[11] Eric Ravenscraft, "Why the FCC's New Net Neutrality Rules Are Good for the Internet," Lifehacker, February 26, 2015, http://lifehacker.com/why-the-fccs-new-net-neutrality-rules-are-good-for-the-1683769527.

[12] Patti M. Valkenburg and Jochen Peter, "Social Consequences of the Internet for Adolescents A Decade of Research," *Current Directions in Psychological Science* 18, no. 1 (February 1, 2009): 1–5, https://doi.org/10.1111/j.1467-8721.2009.01595.x.

[13] Emily C. Weinstein and Robert L. Selman, "Digital Stress: Adolescents' Personal Accounts," *New Media & Society* 18, no. 3 (March 1, 2016): 391–409, https://doi.org/10.1177/1461444814543989.

[14] Ibid.

[15] Emily C. Weinstein et al., "How to Cope With Digital Stress The Recommendations Adolescents Offer Their Peers Online," *Journal of Adolescent*

Because of the rise of the Internet and the prevalence of Internet-related incidents, school officials face enormous pressure to do something (or to act) when actions are necessary. However, school interventions do not always work out as intended. Similar interventions seldom yield positive results for school districts and school administrators. Every action or conduct, which is committed or omitted by school personnel, often has dire consequences. Legal disputes are among the most common downsides of school interventions in any incidents. School interventions can be even more precarious in online incidents. It is always best for schools to tread with caution.

From a technical lens, how to best apprehend cyberbullying? The answer might surprise you. Not much is known about this trend. What might explain the nature of that incongruity, considering that this type of online misconduct is common across the United States? The literature is ambivalent about the conduct, which can be described as online bullying.

Research, June 18, 2015, 0743558415587326, https://doi.org/10.1177/0743558415587326.

3

A LACK OF CLEAR DEFINITIONS

Online bullying, also known as cyberbullying, is a prying behavior, sometimes a destructive attitude, if not a devastating conduct, which can cause emotional, psychological, and even mental distress. It is the electronic evolution of face-to-face bullying, which is widespread among children and adolescents.[1] Research shows that online bullying is expected to thrive among

---

[1] Anna Costanza Baldry, David P Farrington, and Anna Sorrentino, "'Am I at Risk of Cyberbullying'? A Narrative Review and Conceptual Framework for Research on Risk of Cyberbullying and Cybervictimization: The Risk and Needs Assessment Approach," *Aggression and Violent Behavior* 23 (2015): 36–51; Fabio Sticca, "Bullying Goes Online: Definition, Risk Factors, Consequences, and Prevention of (Cyber) Bullying," 2013.

students with issues related to psychosocial, affective, and academic problems.[2] Bullying is a national health problem.[3] It is an important social concern.[4]

Amid the presumed surge of bullying incidents, observers have called for actions. Others have flat out demanded that authorities eradicate the practice. However, this is a tall order pursuit.

Despite the harmful nature of bullying and the fact that such a practice has been around for decades, modern societies have not been able to curtail similar practices. This reality is even more blatant when it comes to online bullying. The reason is that it is always possible to identify perpetrators. Else, it is challenging to know the rate of victimization as few people report such occurrences to local authorities. It might be unrealistic to abolish bullying. It may be impossible to stop people from engaging in a similar misconduct. This is true regardless of the frequency of incidents and their locus of occurrence.

***

There are various types of cyberbullying.[5] These activities occur through various means, including text messages, instant messaging, e-mail communications, phone calls, and pictures/video clips, chat

---

[2] Tokunaga, "Following You Home from School: A Critical Review and Synthesis of Research on Cyberbullying Victimization."

[3] Juvonen and Gross, "Extending the School Grounds?—Bullying Experiences in Cyberspace."

[4] Patchin and Hinduja, "Bullies Move beyond the Schoolyard: A Preliminary Look at Cyberbullying."

[5] Slonje and Smith, "Cyberbullying: Another Main Type of Bullying?"

rooms, or websites, although text messages can be more prevalent in online bullying incidents.[6] The most frequent forms of online incidents are more likely to take place through instant messaging.[7] People who have experienced online bullying may also develop low self-esteem.

The bulk of online bullying occurs off school grounds.[8] Online bullying victims may become susceptible to depression; they may even harbor suicidal feelings. The effects of online bullying can be incommensurable in a person's psyche. Cyberbullying is a psychosocial experience. It may cause emotional and physical distress for a person.

Online bullying is not a recent phenomenon. Face-to-face bullying preceded online bullying. This form of bullying is known as "traditional bullying." This facet of bullying involves behaviors that may be physical or psychological, designed to bully, harass, and intimidate others.

Cyberbullying is intrusive. It is a form of psychological abuse that can cause mental problems, many of which can be associated with suicidal inclinations.[9] Observers consider online bullying to

---

[6] Kowalski and Limber, "Electronic Bullying among Middle School Students"; Slonje and Smith, "Cyberbullying: Another Main Type of Bullying?"; Smith et al., "Cyberbullying: Its Nature and Impact in Secondary School Pupils."

[7] Juvonen and Gross, "Extending the School Grounds?—Bullying Experiences in Cyberspace."

[8] Smith et al., "Cyberbullying: Its Nature and Impact in Secondary School Pupils."

[9] Djedjiga Mouheb et al., "Real-Time Detection of Cyberbullying in Arabic Twitter Streams" (2019 10th IFIP International Conference on New Technologies, Mobility and Security (NTMS), IEEE, 2019), 1–5.

be more conspicuous than face-to-face misconduct. It is dangerous and affects children and adolescents.[10]

Online bullying could lead to unpleasant moments. It is usually more complex than the way critics paint the problem. This category of bullying can devastate the victim. It is important to identify those at risk as early as possible and develop interventions.[11]

***

Cyberbullying poses a greater threat to students, as opposed to a traditional (or ordinary) harassment experience, which has no preference for victims. Cyberbullying victims are always targeted. Thus, this type of aggression is seldom a random act.

This category of bullying can have damaging effects on the victim. It may exceed the expectations of the perpetrator. Experiencing or observing similar incidents can have devastating effects on a person's psyche. School actions (or the lack of that) could have immeasurable effects. Identifying online bullying can be problematic. Addressing electronic bullying can be more complex than most people realize.

Although the idea of bullying is not exogenous, it can be a daunting task to address online misdeeds and the issues that usually breed a similar behavior. One reason that might explain

---

[10] Ibid.

[11] Baldry, Farrington, and Sorrentino, "'Am I at Risk of Cyberbullying'? A Narrative Review and Conceptual Framework for Research on Risk of Cyberbullying and Cybervictimization: The Risk and Needs Assessment Approach."

such a reality is that the nature of online victimization (as a stand-alone happening) is confusing to most observers. Popular arguments debating the roots of this phenomenon may be in error. Similar points of strife may invite criticism and other forms of rebuke. It is important to grasp the essentiality of cyberbullying in terms of its characteristics and features.

4

THE NATURE OF CYBERBULLYING

Although cyberbullying is a major dilemma, which many American school districts face in their quotidian, it has also been the subject of intense media scrutiny.[1] This occurrence is prevalent both inside and outside the school.[2] Scholars and school professionals consider online bullying as a spinoff of the old schoolyard bullying, also known as traditional bullying.

There is an intricate relationship between traditional

---

[1] Julian J Dooley, Jacek Pyżalski, and Donna Cross, "Cyberbullying versus Face-to-Face Bullying: A Theoretical and Conceptual Review.," *Zeitschrift Für Psychologie/Journal of Psychology* 217, no. 4 (2009): 182.

[2] Smith et al., "Cyberbullying: Its Nature and Impact in Secondary School Pupils."

harassment and electronic bullying,[3] although the common understanding is that cyberbullying is perceived as more virulent than face-to-face harassment.[4] The literature is ambivalent about the theoretical and conceptual underpinnings of the phenomenon.[5]

As a new social happening, online bullying has received increased scholarly scrutiny.[6] There had been many studies on electronic bullying. For many scholars, the phenomenon represents a significant problem, though it is not well understood. This problem will not go away even with implementing anti-bullying programs in schools.[7] However, online bullying has become more problematic over the years, notably over the past decade.[8]

The presumption is that school officials cannot intervene when incidents occur. Of course, this understanding could not be further from the truth. If fact, the opposite reality is likely to be the case in various school districts across the United States.

***

---

[3] Raskauskas and Stoltz, "Involvement in Traditional and Electronic Bullying among Adolescents."

[4] Sticca, "Bullying Goes Online: Definition, Risk Factors, Consequences, and Prevention of (Cyber) Bullying."

[5] Dooley, Pyżalski, and Cross, "Cyberbullying versus Face-to-Face Bullying: A Theoretical and Conceptual Review."

[6] Patchin and Hinduja, "Bullies Move beyond the Schoolyard: A Preliminary Look at Cyberbullying."

[7] Ken Rigby, "What Can Schools Do about Cases of Bullying?," *Pastoral Care in Education* 29, no. 4 (2011): 273–85.

[8] Cindy L Corliss, "The Established and the Outsiders: Cyberbullying as an Exclusionary Process," 2017.

Online bullying, many observers are convinced, is out of control. Internet misconduct is a matter of concern for students, teachers, and parents.[9] Bullying has led to several tragic deaths of teens.[10] The phenomenon is prevalent among school-age children. A gender component in this occurrence is also noteworthy.

Although males are envisioned as bullies, females are likely to become cyberbullies.[11] A study found that 60% of cyberbullying victims are women.[12] A little over 52% of victims are males.[13] The most prevalent forms of online bullying include name-calling or insults.[14] School administrators are reluctant to take actions for fear of reprisal from parents.

With interventions, school professionals have a genuine fear of legal repercussions. School officials are afraid of lawsuits from parents and students. School districts often find themselves at the mercy of court rulings, which, in the past, were to be expected to favor students.

Although it may be pointless to deny that online bullying is real and affects both students and parents, there is an enormous gap in the literature about the extent of the problem of school

---

[9] Ryan, "The Internet Playground: One School's Experience of Cyberbullying."

[10] Dooley, Pyżalski, and Cross, "Cyberbullying versus Face-to-Face Bullying: A Theoretical and Conceptual Review."

[11] Li, "Cyberbullying in Schools: A Research of Gender Differences."

[12] Li, "New Bottle but Old Wine: A Research of Cyberbullying in Schools."

[13] Ibid.

[14] Juvonen and Gross, "Extending the School Grounds?—Bullying Experiences in Cyberspace."

interventions in such issues. Bullying is a negative by-product of recent social changes toward digital communication. [15] Little is known about bullying activities in schools or in the cyberspace. Despite intense media attention to the problem during the last decade, little is known about cyberbullying. [16] There are not enough debates in the literature on how to solve the problem.

No one would challenge the notion that cyberbullying has material effects on society. Although this occurrence is a virtual phenomenon, it has real-world consequences. [17] It includes a variety of behaviors.[18] Bullying has real-life self-esteem effects on children, making them vulnerable to becoming victimized by bullies.[19]

Observers believe that electronic bullying is on the rise in various school districts. Rigby and Smith (2011) wondered whether bullying in schools had increased in recent years. They noted that such an understanding is common in various media

---

[15] Sticca, "Bullying Goes Online: Definition, Risk Factors, Consequences, and Prevention of (Cyber) Bullying."

[16] Dooley, Pyżalski, and Cross, "Cyberbullying versus Face-to-Face Bullying: A Theoretical and Conceptual Review."; Sticca, "Bullying Goes Online: Definition, Risk Factors, Consequences, and Prevention of (Cyber) Bullying."

[17] TS Sathyanarayana Rao, Deepali Bansal, and Suhas Chandran, "Cyberbullying: A Virtual Offense with Real Consequences," *Indian Journal of Psychiatry* 60, no. 1 (2018): 3.

[18] Sticca, "Bullying Goes Online: Definition, Risk Factors, Consequences, and Prevention of (Cyber) Bullying."

[19] AAL Kuipers, "Real Life Social Self-Esteem Affects Children's Likelihood to Be a Victim of Cyberbullying.," 2018.

sources.[20] The rise of similar incidents is often echoed by popular commentators. However, the prevalence of the bullying phenomenon in school settings or elsewhere remains unclear.

---

[20] Ken Rigby and Peter K Smith, "Is School Bullying Really on the Rise?," *Social Psychology of Education* 14, no. 4 (2011): 441–55.

5

STUDENT MISBEHAVING ONLINE

How often do you think students misbehave on the Internet? How prevalent is online bullying? Answers may come across as too convoluted or even too confusing to make a defined prognostic of this occurrence.

It is undeniable that traditional behaviors can easily manifest themselves through online conduct. Physical and verbal bullying can easily turn into online bullying activities.[1] Studies found that online bullying can be less frequent than traditional bullying.[2]

---

[1] Kirk R Williams and Nancy G Guerra, "Prevalence and Predictors of Internet Bullying," *Journal of Adolescent Health* 41, no. 6 (2007): S14–21.

[2] Smith et al., "Cyberbullying: Its Nature and Impact in Secondary School Pupils."

Another study found that 54% of students were victimized by traditional bullying. [3] However, a quarter of those students experienced electronic harassment. [4] Even those who had been bullied also knew someone else who had been bullied. [5] It is a cycle of harassment, which few adolescents or fewer school-age children could escape.

The conversation about online bullying can be fierce. Viewpoints diverge on the roots of student behavior. This is in part because the nuances and similarities between online and face-to-face bullying are not well established in the literature. [6]

It is unquestionable that intervening in bullying-related offenses is increasingly becoming a major problem for school administrators. But the line between face-to-face harassment and electronic bullying can be blurry. Hence, the right course of action is not always obvious to school officials.

***

Verbal bullying is the precursor of online bullying. [7] But online bullying could easily turn into face-to-face aggressions. Although verbal incidents peak in middle school, they are prophesied to

---

[3] Li, "New Bottle but Old Wine: A Research of Cyberbullying in Schools."

[4] Ibid.

[5] Li, "Cyberbullying in Schools: A Research of Gender Differences."

[6] Dooley, Pyżalski, and Cross, "Cyberbullying versus Face-to-Face Bullying: A Theoretical and Conceptual Review."

[7] Williams and Guerra, "Prevalence and Predictors of Internet Bullying."

remain elevated throughout high school.[8] Verbal incidents are also prevalent in middle schools. [9] They are usually followed by physical bullying incidents, which subside in high school.[10]

Most cyberbullying incidents were perpetrated by one or a few students.[11] A study found that about two-thirds of online bullying victims knew their perpetrators. [12] It was usually someone that students knew from school. [13] This reality could easily be explained, since the Internet is ubiquitous in student lives.

The increased availability of electronic communication technologies, namely the Internet and mobile phones, made it possible for adolescents to bully one another in complete impunity.[14] In its traditional form, bullying is even more prevalent than most people realize. One in three students engaged in a traditional form of bullying.[15] Similarly, 15% of students have used the Internet to bully others. [16] Despite this reality, it may be

---

[8] Ibid.

[9] Ibid.

[10] Ibid.

[11] Smith et al., "Cyberbullying: Its Nature and Impact in Secondary School Pupils."

[12] Juvonen and Gross, "Extending the School Grounds?—Bullying Experiences in Cyberspace."

[13] Ibid.

[14] Kowalski and Limber, "Electronic Bullying among Middle School Students"; Raskauskas and Stoltz, "Involvement in Traditional and Electronic Bullying among Adolescents."

[15] Li, "New Bottle but Old Wine: A Research of Cyberbullying in Schools."

[16] Ibid.

impossible for students to escape technologies related to the Internet. In the same way, it may be impossible for students to avoid bullying in one form or another.

***

Nowadays, most people have access to the Internet or similar technologies. Adolescents are very active on social media networks, including Twitter and Facebook,[17] which, as of November 2022, Facebook reported over 2.2 million unique monthly visitors. [18] Correspondingly, most students carry a smart phone; else, they possess other devices from which they could access the web. But communications on social media are not always negative.[19]

An important implication of the unsettling trend about online bullying is worth noting. There may not be a way to reduce student interactions in the cyberspace. We may not prevent or deter students from misbehaving on the Internet. Such a plausibility also means that most people might find it difficult to be safe from aggressions or they may find it hard to escape from their online aggressors.

In summary, the popularity of the Internet does not bode well

---

[17] Anastasio Ovejero et al., "Cyberbullying: Definitions and Facts from a Psychosocial Perspective," in *Cyberbullying across the Globe* (Springer, 2016), 1–31.

[18] eBizMBA, "Top 15 Most Popular Social Networking Sites," eBizMBA, November 2022, http://www.ebizmba.com/articles/social-networking-websites.

[19] Paul Benjamin Lowry et al., "Why Do Adults Engage in Cyberbullying on Social Media? An Integration of Online Disinhibition and Deindividuation Effects with the Social Structure and Social Learning Model," *Information Systems Research* 27, no. 4 (2016): 962–86.

for many people, notably children. Cyberbullying is related to general Internet use.[20] The Internet can be a dangerous place for most people. While children are vulnerable in the cyberspace, it is widely understood that most students also misbehave on the Internet. Children, most times, are both the victims and the perpetrators of online aggressions, which makes the problem of online bullying even more difficult to address. In the same way, this reality renders school response to similar incidents highly contentious both administratively and legally.

---

[20] Smith et al., "Cyberbullying: Its Nature and Impact in Secondary School Pupils."

Part Two: The Need for School Actions

Keywords: School intervention, reporting incidents, eliminate bullying, better policies, being initiative taking, dealing with cyberbullies.

6

REPORTING ONLINE CONDUCT

In modern societies, most ordinary forms of personal communications among individuals take place on the Internet. That interaction[1] can turn ugly. People can be cruel to others.

When people despise one another, they may go to great lengths to manifest that hatred. They may do so in diverse ways. When a troubled person feels the need to harass another, there may be little school officials can do to prevent such an aggression. When two or more of these individuals feel the need to express their misgivings to another student, they often have no restraint to act. They may

---

[1] If one could refer to it that way.

even do so in public. Their weapon of choice can be understood as bullying, which can take place online or in the schoolyard.

Because of the rise of Internet-related technologies, people may not be deterred from expressing their hatred for others. They may do so in the cyberspace. That manifestation may lead to harassment, stalking, and bullying, among other acts. But the conduct of bullying itself, as a form of online misconduct, may be described, at least at prima facia, cyberbullying.

In deciphering a bullying act or a conduct, be it a face-to-face incident or online, the line between offenders and victims can be blurry. In general, the bully is fictitious in nature. He or she is a stock character from a popular television shows or movies. [2] However, in school settings, the original bully is a troubled schoolchild, usually a misguided boy or a tormented girl. But the act of bullying itself, some might say, cannot go unnoticed. It is the business of school officials to respond to similar activities accordingly.

***

Bullying, as a dangerous conduct, is prevalent in schools, particularly in North American schools, including the United States and Canada. In America, for example, students do not always get along. They often target each other on school grounds. Nowadays,

---

[2] Joanne Laucius, "Why Some Victims Become Bullies: Q&A with Bullying Expert Tracy Vaillancourt," Ottawa Citizen, November 23, 2014, http://ottawacitizen.com/news/local-news/why-some-victims-become-bullies-qa-with-bullying-expert-tracy-vaillancourt.

this reality has worsened. The Internet provides students with a venue to vent their frustration towards others, except that they not only have the schoolyard to harass another student, but they also have the cyberspace.

The debate is raging about the reason students misbehave online. There is no consensus in the literature. Understandably, not much is known about the reason (or the potential reasons), which might explain such a reality.

A vital question to pose here is why students misbehave online? When they do, why would school officials not punish them? Are school officials powerless to intervene in online bullying incidents?

To answer these questions, we need to gather three pieces of information. First, we need to know when the incident occurred. Second, we need to separate the perpetrator from the victim. Third, we need to have a logical strategy to address the problem at its core. However, accomplishing these tasks might be more complex than you think. Containing student conduct online might be easier said than done.

***

It is unequivocal that students engage in online bullying. They do so more often than most people realize. A bullying incident can last for about a week.[3] It may also last longer, which can be over a year.[4] However, that information is not always available to school

---

[3] Smith et al., "Cyberbullying: Its Nature and Impact in Secondary School Pupils."

[4] Ibid.

officials. Students do not always report their bullying experiences. They can be even more secretive about online bullying.

The degree to which students are defenseless online is also unclear. A growing school of thought suggests that students can be both the aggressors and the victims of online aggressions.[5] There is also a relationship between online bullying and traditional bullying.[6] Most victims of cyberbullying used to experience a similar harassment tactic in the schoolyard.

***

Experiencing bullying on the Internet can lead to being bullied at school.[7] Most cyberbullying victims were also victims of face-to-face bullying,[8] although those who were victimized in the schoolyard were less fit to become online bullies themselves.[9] Notwithstanding the reality of bullying, those who have been victimized online are not likely to report the incident.[10]

Most of the students who experienced an online harassment, even bystanders, did not report the incidents to adults.[11] A study

---

[5] Ibid.

[6] Raskauskas and Stoltz, "Involvement in Traditional and Electronic Bullying among Adolescents."

[7] Ibid.

[8] Smith et al., "Cyberbullying: Its Nature and Impact in Secondary School Pupils."

[9] Raskauskas and Stoltz, "Involvement in Traditional and Electronic Bullying among Adolescents."

[10] Li, "New Bottle but Old Wine: A Research of Cyberbullying in Schools"; Smith et al., "Cyberbullying: Its Nature and Impact in Secondary School Pupils."

[11] Li, "New Bottle but Old Wine: A Research of Cyberbullying in Schools."

found that 90% of victims did not tell an adult about the cyberbullying incident.[12] Of the percentage of people who report their experience of bullying to adults, there is a gender difference. With experience of bullying, women victims of cyberbullying are inclined to report the incident.[13] Whereas male victims are more abeyant to keep their experience to themselves. School officials often make up the only form of authorities that could protect students from themselves in the cyberspace.

It is undeniable that online bullying is a popular affair in the US. This form of bullying can be destructive. It is harassment to the greatest extent it is demeaning; it is degrading; it is demoralizing. Online bullying is pervasive; it is offensive.

***

Most observers see cyber-criminality as a global problem. This type of criminality differs from the computer crimes that existed in the 1960s and 1970s.[14] It is a threat to Internet-based entities, including business and other forms of enterprises that rely on Internet technologies, namely schools, colleges, institutes, and computer centers, to name a few.[15] Manifested as cyberbullying,

---

[12] Juvonen and Gross, "Extending the School Grounds?—Bullying Experiences in Cyberspace."

[13] Li, "Cyberbullying in Schools: A Research of Gender Differences."

[14] Susan W Brenner, *Cybercrime: Criminal Threats from Cyberspace* (ABC-CLIO, 2010).

[15] Mohan Krishna Kagita et al., "A Review on Cyber Crimes on the Internet of Things," *Deep Learning for Security and Privacy Preservation in IoT*, 2021, 83–98.

the Internet poses a serious threat to youth in the digital age.[16] The problem remains the same. How to address this issue? There is no definite answer.

It is irrefutable that cyber criminality affects students.[17] Still, it may be difficult to locate cyber offenders. The manner in which school officials address the problem may be even more problematic.

Views on the extent of electronic bullying may be inaccurate. Such misapprehension may lead to inaccurate disciplinary measures. There is no cure for online misconduct. It is difficult to determine who the perpetrators are. Cyberbullies are anonymous. They may hide their online identity through various means.

In sum, online-related crimes are on the rise in the world. Cyberbullying is among the most virulent crimes that occur on the Internet. But identifying cybercriminals is not always easy. Therefore, detecting online bullying can be difficult.

---

[16] Nilüfer Sezer and Serdar Tunçer, "Cyberbullying Hurts: The Rising Threat to Youth in the Digital Age," *Digital Siege (Ss. 179-194). Istanbul: Istanbul University Press. Https://Doi. Org/10.26650/B/SS07* 9 (2021).

[17] MH Abdul-Rahim, "Assessment of the Perceptions on the Effects of Cybercrime on Senior High Students in Tamale Metropolis: A Case Study of Vitting Senior High School" (The University for Development Studies, 2021), http://41.66.217.101/handle/123456789/2976.

7

THE NEED TO ERADICATE BULLYING

To what extent is online bullying common in schools? There is no definite answer. The unique features of electronic communication have given rise to a virulent form of bullying on the Internet.[1] But there is not much verity in that viewpoint. The pervasiveness of cyberbullying could easily be exaggerated. Concerns about the prevalence of school bullying could be attributed to popular perceptions, which often differ from actual

---

[1] Jaana Juvonen and Sandra Graham, "Bullying in Schools: The Power of Bullies and the Plight of Victims," *Annual Review of Psychology* 65, no. 1 (2014): 159–85.

rates of bullying incidents.[2]

Observers have wondered what could be done to address the rise of bullying cases in schools.[3] The prevalent view is that schools could not punish students for cyberbullying.[4] But this is far from the truth.

In response to electronic bullying activities, many schools have adopted a zero-tolerance approach. Most of the time, they did so as a deterrence tactic to prevent students from wreaking havoc online. The goal is to deal with the problem in its roots. For most school officials, online bullying is a nuisance that must be addressed immediately and swiftly. Despite the endless rise of research on school bullying worldwide, important facets of the problem remain unclear.[5]

School officials assess harsh punishments to students who engage in Internet exchanges, which students, parents, or school staff members consider questionable. The debate over the reason for harsh punishments is raging. In 2011, Waldman argued against criminalizing traditional and electronic bullying. The author

---

[2] Evelyn M Campbell and Susan E Smalling, "American Indians and Bullying in Schools," 2013.

[3] Rigby, "What Can Schools Do about Cases of Bullying?"

[4] Rachel Young, Melissa Tully, and Marizen Ramirez, "School Administrator Perceptions of Cyberbullying Facilitators and Barriers to Preventive Action: A Qualitative Study," *Health Education & Behavior* 44, no. 3 (2017): 476–84.

[5] Ken Rigby, "School Perspectives on Bullying and Preventative Strategies: An Exploratory Study," *Australian Journal of Education* 61, no. 1 (2017): 24–39.

considers harsh criminal punishments for bullying egregious.[6] The consensus is that school should have a clear policy in place to guide punishment. [7] Anti-cyberbullying policies must be included in official school rules.[8]

***

When students engage in lewd or offensive conduct, school administrators are quick to sanction the student (or the students) involved. Punitive sanctions for online misconduct can range from a mere verbal warning to full-blown student expulsion from the school. There may be no formal recourse against the disciplinary actions taken by school administrators. There lies another problem. Schools do not always have clear policy recommendations in place to guide administrative actions.

Most observers believe that schools should enact specific policies to discourage bullying and cyberbullying.[9] School officials are concerned about the accusation that they should not criminalize cyberbullying.[10] In recent years, there have been calls to outlaw cyberbullying. Criminal punishments for students who

---

6 Ari Ezra Waldman, "Tormented: Antigay Bullying in Schools," *Temp. L. Rev.* 84 (2011): 385.

7 Sameer Hinduja and Justin W Patchin, "State Cyberbullying Laws," *Cyberbullying Research Center*, 2012.

8 Alvin J Primack and Kevin A Johnson, "Student Cyberbullying inside the Digital Schoolhouse Gate: Toward a Standard for Determining Where a 'School' Is," *First Amendment Studies* 51, no. 1 (2017): 30–48.

9 Hinduja and Patchin, "State Cyberbullying Laws."

10 Lyrissa Lidsky and Andrea Pinzon Garcia, "How Not to Criminalize Cyberbullying," *Mo. L. Rev.* 77 (2012): 693.

cyberbully others are considered an alternative form of punishment.[11] Another problem is worthy of note here as well.

Another belief is that school districts must find a constitutional avenue to combat cyberbullying. [12] Schools can aggressively punish students for electronic bullying within the purview of the First Amendment. [13] Barring any violation of First Amendment rights, school authorities can punish students for speech, even though such a speech may have originally been created off-school grounds.[14]

In online incidents, interventions can be arbitrary; they can be impulsive. The affirmed perpetrator may have little or no means of defending himself. The student is minded, in most cases, to endure a barrage of insults, which may lead to public shaming. But this can go against legal standards. In Tinker v. Des Moines Independent Community School District, the Supreme Court notes that a school may punish student expression.[15]

---

[11] James L Seay III, "Salvaging the North Carolina Teacher-Cyberbullying Statute," *Campbell L. Rev.* 37 (2015): 391.

[12] Naomi Harlin Goodno, "How Public Schools Can Constitutionally Halt Cyberbullying: A Model Cyberbullying Policy That Considers First Amendment, Due Process, and Fourth Amendment Challenges," *Wake Forest L. Rev.* 46 (2011): 641.

[13] Darcy K Lane, "Taking the Lead on Cyberbullying: Why Schools Can and Should Protect Students Online," *Iowa L. Rev.* 96 (2010): 1791.

[14] Y Tony Yang and Erin Grinshteyn, "Safer Cyberspace through Legal Intervention: A Comparative Review of Cyberbullying Legislation," *World Medical & Health Policy* 8, no. 4 (2016): 458–77.

[15] Tinker v. Des Moines Independent Community School Dist., 393 US 503 (Supreme Court 1969).

***

The Tinker standard is still relevant today. As of 2021, there is no ambivalence about student rights in schools. A school can punish a student for his or her online behavior.[16] But school policies must not be vague; they must not invite arbitrary actions.[17]

With corrective actions taken by school officials during online misconduct, students and parents may find themselves in a limbo. This experience can be a nightmare for students. School officials are seldom forgiving in their resolution of a (possible) online problem. Parents often have no alternative but to take legal action against the school. Parents are increasingly choosing to sue schools.[18]

With aggrieved parents, the tendency is to sue cyberbully parents.[19] This approach is not always productive. Parents always end up suing schools.[20] They are not ostensibly pleased with the disciplinary reach of the school administration. They may be unhappy with school interventions for incidents that (allegedly) occurred outside school grounds. Students may have no choice but

---

[16] Aliya Kintonova, Alexander Vasyaev, and Viktor Shestak, "Cyberbullying and Cyber-Mobbing in Developing Countries," *Information & Computer Security*, 2021.

[17] Shaheen Shariff and Dianne L Hoff, "Cyber Bullying: Clarifying Legal Boundaries for School Supervision in Cyberspace," 2016.

[18] Ibid.

[19] Ryan Broll, "Collaborative Responses to Cyberbullying: Preventing and Responding to Cyberbullying through Nodes and Clusters," *Policing and Society* 26, no. 7 (2016): 735–52; Des Butler, "Cyberbullying and the Law: Parameters for Effective Interventions?," in *Reducing Cyberbullying in Schools* (Elsevier, 2018), 49–60.

[20] Butler, "Cyberbullying and the Law: Parameters for Effective Interventions?"

to sue the school or even school officials; they are sometimes named directly in the complaint.

Taking legal actions against the school (or school officials) often becomes a source of comfort, which disgruntled parents could consider against what some observers regularly label as vague, arbitrary, or unpredictable disciplinary measures. Legal actions may be the only way parents (and students) can express their concerns about school policies (or the lack of that) addressing online behaviors, which, most of the time, took place off school grounds. This is the essentiality of the debate about school interventions.

8

SCHOOL INTERVENTIONS AND EXISTING POLICIES

The presumption is that bullying cases are increasing. This is a major concern across the United States. But this is not just an American issue. Bullying is a major problem in schools around the world.[1]

Bullying is a pervasive type of aggression, which affects schools.[2]

---

[1] Ken Rigby and Kaye Johnson, *The Prevalence and Effectiveness of Anti-Bullying Strategies Employed in Australian Schools* (University of South Australia Adelaide, 2016).

[2] Alana James, "School Bullying," *Res Briefing Nedlastet Fra Www Nspcc Org Uk/Inform* 26 (2010): 2012.

It can be both reactive and proactive violence.[3] Bullying is a type of belligerence; it is both hostile and proactive.[4]

Every country in the world, which had been surveyed, has some bullying.[5] It is well understood that schools can fend off bullying conduct by adopting whole-school anti-bullying policies.[6] The common belief is that school officials struggle to address online bullying. Many believe that this is in part because courts rarely decide in favor of school districts in online-related litigation.

Observers see an injustice towards school officials when the most important part of their job is to keep the school safe. The measures they must take to ensure school safety can prevent them from being sued. Another explanation is often overlooked in the debate. Not every school has a specific bullying policy. This is an anomaly, as schools must have policies in place to tackle bullying.[7] In some places, this is mandatory. In England, for instance, schools

---

[3] Marina Camodeca et al., "Bullying and Victimization among School-age Children: Stability and Links to Proactive and Reactive Aggression," *Social Development* 11, no. 3 (2002): 332–45; Charles R McAdams III and Christopher D Schmidt, "How to Help a Bully: Recommendations for Counseling the Proactive Aggressor," *Professional School Counseling* 11, no. 2 (2007): 2156759X0701100207.

[4] Mahri J Elinoff, Sandra M Chafouleas, and Kari A Sassu, "Bullying: Considerations for Defining and Intervening in School Settings," *Psychology in the Schools* 41, no. 8 (2004): 887–97.

[5] Rigby and Johnson, *The Prevalence and Effectiveness of Anti-Bullying Strategies Employed in Australian Schools*.

[6] Mike Eslea and Peter K Smith, "The Long-term Effectiveness of Anti-bullying Work in Primary Schools," *Educational Research* 40, no. 2 (1998): 203–18.

[7] Muthanna Samara and Peter K Smith, "How Schools Tackle Bullying, and the Use of Whole School Policies: Changes over the Last Decade," *Educational Psychology* 28, no. 6 (2008): 663–76.

are expected to have an anti-bullying policy.[8]

***

While there is no definite cure to fix online bullying, the best solution, as many critics might say, is for school officials to be real in their response to (known) incidents. Schools must be proactive against bullying.[9] School officials must review and understand their policy guidelines on cyberbullying, particularly their position against harassment and bullying policies.[10]

School officials must develop and update (regularly) their policies on cyberbullying.[11] They must develop the framework to

---

[8] Peter K Smith et al., "A Content Analysis of School Anti-Bullying Policies: A Follow-up after Six Years," *Educational Psychology in Practice* 28, no. 1 (2012): 47–70; Peter K Smith et al., "A Content Analysis of School Anti-bullying Policies: Progress and Limitations," *Educational Psychology in Practice* 24, no. 1 (2008): 1–12.

[9] Jon M Philipson, "Kids Are Not All Right: Mandating Peer Mediation as a Proactive Anti-Bullying Measure in Schools," *Cardozo J. Conflict Resol.* 14 (2012): 81; Robert W Smith and Kayce Smith, "Creating the Cougar Watch: Learning to Be Proactive against Bullying in Schools. Despite Reticence from the Central Office, Strong Middle Level Teacher Leaders Worked Together to Develop an Effective Anti-Bullying Program That Addresses a Significant Need for Safety and Inclusion for All Middle School Students," *Middle School Journal* 46, no. 1 (2014): 13–19; Jeannine R Studer and Blair S Mynatt, "Bullying Prevention in Middle Schools: A Collaborative Approach: Collaborative, Proactive Anti-Bullying Interventions and Policies That Strive to Create and Sustain a Safe Environment for All Adolescents," *Middle School Journal* 46, no. 3 (2015): 25–32.

[10] Justin W Patchin and Sameer Hinduja, "School-Based Efforts to Prevent Cyberbullying," *The Prevention Researcher* 19, no. 3 (2012): 7–10; Russell A. Sabella, Justin W. Patchin, and Sameer Hinduja, "Cyberbullying Myths and Realities," *Computers in Human Behavior* 29, no. 6 (November 1, 2013): 2703–11, https://doi.org/10.1016/j.chb.2013.06.040.

[11] Christine Suniti Bhat, "Cyber Bullying: Overview and Strategies for School Counsellors, Guidance Officers, and All School Personnel," *Journal of Psychologists and Counsellors in Schools* 18, no. 1 (2008): 53–66.

address online incidents. Such a framework must be informed by existing policy guidelines. School officials must ensure that existing policies prohibit cyberbullying in the most explicit terms.[12]

School leaders must be initiative taking; they must be active participants in solving the problem. Proactive strategies can help schools develop anti-bullying initiatives. [13] They must take a collaborative approach.[14] They must develop a suitable mediation technique to address bullying.[15]

It is important for schools to have prevention programs as an attempt to tackle bullying.[16] Anti-bullying programs must improve the school in its entirety.[17] Such programs must be both proactive and preventive to promote student welfare and other activities.[18]

With school interventions when students engage in online

---

[12] Kathleen Conn, "Cyberbullying and Other Student Technology Misuses in K-12 American Schools: The Legal Landmines," *Widener L. Rev.* 16 (2010): 89.

[13] Fran Thompson and Peter K Smith, "The Use and Effectiveness of Anti-Bullying Strategies in Schools," *Research Brief DFE-RR098*, 2011, 1–220.

[14] Studer and Mynatt, "Bullying Prevention in Middle Schools: A Collaborative Approach: Collaborative, Proactive Anti-Bullying Interventions and Policies That Strive to Create and Sustain a Safe Environment for All Adolescents."

[15] Philipson, "Kids Are Not All Right: Mandating Peer Mediation as a Proactive Anti-Bullying Measure in Schools."

[16] John Pitts and Philip Smith, *Preventing School Bullying* (Citeseer, 1995).

[17] Smith and Smith, "Creating the Cougar Watch: Learning to Be Proactive against Bullying in Schools. Despite Reticence from the Central Office, Strong Middle Level Teacher Leaders Worked Together to Develop an Effective Anti-Bullying Program That Addresses a Significant Need for Safety and Inclusion for All Middle School Students."

[18] Annarilla Ahtola, "Proactive and Preventive Student Welfare Activities in Finnish Preschool and Elementary School: Handling of Transition to Formal Schooling and a National Anti-Bullying Program as Examples," 2012.

activities, there is always the potential that school officials might take actions that might have unintended consequences. For example, being too aggressive can be unproductive. Being too passive is also not productive. Therefore, it is important for schools to understand the parameters of their interventions in school settings.[19]

---

[19] Elinoff, Chafouleas, and Sassu, "Bullying: Considerations for Defining and Intervening in School Settings."

9

AN INITIATIVE-TAKING APPROACH

When dealing with incidents that occurred outside the school grounds, there may be administrative hurdles. School officials should not address online incidents out of fear, because of emotions, or based on their sheer impulsions. There can be profound consequences that can be legal. Problems arising from school interventions can also be financial. Therefore, school officials must adopt a proactive anti-bullying measure.[1]

With school interventions on cyberbullying, being too direct

---

[1] Philipson, "Kids Are Not All Right: Mandating Peer Mediation as a Proactive Anti-Bullying Measure in Schools."

could lead to a multitude of problems. This approach could cause unanticipated problems for school administrators. For example, students are of a mind to claim that school officials violated their constitutional rights when they punished them for acts that are protected by the US Constitution. To avoid similar problems, school administrators must consider bullying situations; they must consider the extent of anti-bullying policies, notably cyberbullying policies.[2]

A rule of thumb is that most activities that students take part in while roaming the Internet always falls within the expectations of freedom of speech. Such a speech is guaranteed by the US Constitution. In it lies the crux of the problems facing school officials when they intervene haphazardly in incidents that caused harm to others.

Another rule of thumb to consider is that a school intervention must be guided by the desire to stop disruptive activities on school grounds. The courts are firm in their intervention recommendations. There should be a pedagogical reason for school intervention in student activities. But the activity, on its face, must

---

[2] Studer and Mynatt, "Bullying Prevention in Middle Schools: A Collaborative Approach: Collaborative, Proactive Anti-Bullying Interventions and Policies That Strive to Create and Sustain a Safe Environment for All Adolescents."

be disruptive.[3] The conduct must be defiant and disruptive.[4] We will explore this aspect of the debate in subsequent chapters.

***

Other observers believe that the best way to address cyberbullying is to have specific policies in place. These policies must be informed by intervention and prevention strategies.[5] One could hardly argue to the contrary.

A sensible policy about bullying would guide school officials in their intervention practices. Cyberbullying intervention and prevention programs must be effective.[6] Such an approach would help school officials understand when (or how) to intervene in an online bullying incident. Having the right policy documents to guide school interventions could help make a world of difference.

Do school districts have the right policy in place? Do school officials know how to intervene—safely—in online incidents? Answers can be discouraging. But that assessment, if true, would reflect findings from a survey I conducted many years ago on the

---

[3] Elisa Cantone et al., "Interventions on Bullying and Cyberbullying in Schools: A Systematic Review," *Clinical Practice and Epidemiology in Mental Health: CP & EMH* 11, no. Suppl 1 M4 (2015): 58.

[4] Izabela Zych, Anna C Baldry, and David P Farrington, "School Bullying and Cyberbullying: Prevalence, Characteristics, Outcomes, and Prevention," *Handbook of Behavioral Criminology*, 2017, 113–38.

[5] Ted Feinberg and Nicole Robey, "Cyberbullying: Intervention and Prevention Strategies," *National Association of School Psychologists* 38, no. 4 (2009): 22–24.

[6] Hannah Gaffney et al., "Are Cyberbullying Intervention and Prevention Programs Effective? A Systematic and Meta-Analytical Review," *Aggression and Violent Behavior* 45 (2019): 134–53.

issues.[7]

With cyberbullying interventions, school districts (chiefly, school officials) are regularly in trouble for their actions or the lack of that. They often face instances where they might have to explain why they intervened in an incident. School officials might have to explain why they did not intervene in a particular incident. In both instances, school actions (or school omissions) could lead to an overabundance of problems, which could also have legal effects.

---

[7] See the work titled *Cyberbullying Policies in K-12 Public Education: An Analysis of the Legal Implications of School Interventions* to learn more.

PART THREE: POLICIES ABOUT CYBERBULLYING

Keywords: School administration, constitutional rights, right policy documents, rapid interventions, intervention crisis, and policy guidelines.

10

DEFYING POPULAR VIEWPOINTS

In the United States, school interventions in cyberbullying can be unnecessarily controversial. The assumption is that there is an intervention crisis in online bullying. Schools are reeling from ambivalent court decisions, which provide no guidance for interventions. Is there any truth to that assertion? The answer is no.

Observers argue that the law defining school interventions in cyberbullying is not clear. Whenever students claim that school interventions violated their freedom to express the self or other constitutional violations, the courts are predisposed to side with students. This reality often poses a severe problem for school officials. However, this argument does not consider the jurisprudence on the matter. The courts are unequivocal in this issue. School interventions are allowed, provided there is a material disruption of school operations.

School actions involving disciplinary measures are always contentious. There is always the potential for lawsuits or other administrative hurdles when school officials take disciplinary actions against students. The same is true for cyberbullying.

The widely held belief is that school officials must always address incidents related to online offenses notably those perpetrated by students. Such interventions can occur on several levels.[1] They must be practical; they must be relentless; they must be unforgiving. The proposed approach is necessary.

***

Every online bullying conduct has consequences. Similar acts may pose an enormous risk of harm to others. Despite the positive aspects of the Internet, it represents a serious risk to young people.[2] Swift interventions can be important. But the inability of school officials to act quickly could be disastrous.

Rapid school interventions can prevent a student from hurting himself or even hurting others. Most victims of online bullying are susceptible to commit suicide. A lot may weigh in the balance. For example, lives might be at risk when school officials did not

---

[1] Cantone et al., "Interventions on Bullying and Cyberbullying in Schools: A Systematic Review."

[2] Ovejero et al., "Cyberbullying: Definitions and Facts from a Psychosocial Perspective."

intervene. In the same way, intervening unsystematic in cyberbullying incidents may prove financially costly for school officials.

Critics might argue that it is important for school officials to intervene quickly and effectively when they know that a student misbehaved online. Some schools have even adopted a zero-tolerance approach. However, such a strategy may come at a price. This usually involves the cost of dealing with legal disputes. Apart from the economic responsibilities noted above, which characterize litigation in cyber-related school interventions, schools may have to deal with unfair media attention, which may lead to unnecessary public scrutiny, which can lead to fervent criticisms.

Despite the legal implications related to cyberbullying, not intervening in an online incident can have administrative complications. It may have important ethical implications for school administrators. This work, to echo, proposes a simpler approach in the debate. For the sake of literary cogency, the present dialogue does not examine these issues at length.

11

THE EXTENT OF THE INTERVENTION CRISIS

For most school officials, there is an intervention crisis in cyberbullying. The phenomenon itself represents a different type of school crisis.[1] Students are in danger. Compared to other students in schools, those who experienced cyberbullying face a greater risk of depressive symptoms, suicidal ideation, self-injury, and suicide attempt.[2] Even when they are armed with that

---

[1] Salman Elbedour et al., "Cyberbullying: Roles of School Psychologists and School Counselors in Addressing a Pervasive Social Justice Issue," *Children and Youth Services Review* 109 (2020): 104720.

[2] Brenda K Wiederhold, "Cyberbullying and LGBTQ Youth: A Deadly Combination," *Cyberpsychology, Behavior, and Social Networking* 17, no. 9 (2014): 569–70.

knowledge, school officials are *at the drop of hat* ready to take a hasty approach when they found out that students misbehave online. They are also professed to be involved in complex lawsuits.

There are some misconceptions about cyberbullying and school interventions. There are those who do not see online bullying as a problem worthy of addressing.[3] These individuals might claim that their hands are tied. They have few alternatives to fixing the problem. Effective actions to solve the problem are rare. For school professionals, there is no way to address student behavior online. They are, as you might infer from the previous understanding, working in the dark.

There is no need to debate the validity of ideas suggesting that school districts have no real recourse to online bullying. But it is conceivable that most school officials do not have a clear policy guideline, which would help them intervene on similar issues. School policies that can effectively address cyberbullying are important.[4]

***

With online bullying, the line between being professional and being emotional can be fuzzy. Some school officials (inarguably) are guessing on the right techniques to use or the proper strategies to

---

[3] Sterling Stauffer et al., "High School Teachers' Perceptions of Cyberbullying Prevention and Intervention Strategies," *Psychology in the Schools* 49, no. 4 (2012): 352–67.

[4] Elbedour et al., "Cyberbullying: Roles of School Psychologists and School Counselors in Addressing a Pervasive Social Justice Issue."

use when they intervene in online incidents. School officials are also expected to face internal pressures to exercise clear leadership on similar issues.

The reality of school interventions, at least with online bullying, can be complex. Cyberbullying is increasingly becoming a challenge for schools.[5] There is no silver bullet (in a manner of speaking) that could allow school professionals to intervene safely in every online incident. But the harm from cyberbullying is a cause of concern among students.[6]

Parents and students are less prone to praise school interventions that do not consider the ramifications of disciplinary actions. They must also consider that anti-bullying interventions are important in preventing suicide among adolescents. [7] However, parents and students are in the habit of disapproving school actions that are disproportionate and inconsiderate of victims and asserted perpetrators.

School interventions must be potentially helpful.[8] In that case, intervention strategies to address cyberbullying in schools must be

---

[5] Nandoli Von Marées and Franz Petermann, "Cyberbullying: An Increasing Challenge for Schools," *School Psychology International* 33, no. 5 (2012): 467–76.

[6] Carrie-Anne Myers and Helen Cowie, "Cyberbullying across the Lifespan of Education: Issues and Interventions from School to University," *International Journal of Environmental Research and Public Health* 16, no. 7 (2019): 1217.

[7] Apolinaras Zaborskis et al., "The Association between Cyberbullying, School Bullying, and Suicidality among Adolescents: Findings from the Cross-National Study HBSC in Israel, Lithuania, and Luxembourg.," *Crisis: The Journal of Crisis Intervention and Suicide Prevention* 40, no. 2 (2019): 100.

[8] Myers and Cowie, "Cyberbullying across the Lifespan of Education: Issues and Interventions from School to University."

sensible.[9] School officials must endeavor to transform neutral and positive viewpoints about cyberbullying into negative attitudes.[10] The idea is to get people involved to fight this scourge effectively.

A school response to online bullying must incorporate prevention and intervention for better results.[11] It is important that school personnel understand the implications of cyberbullying.[12] The best practices for bullying prevention and intervention include training school personnel.[13] The entire school community must realize the impact of cyberbullying.[14] They must grasp the psychological implications of the singularity.[15] School interventions must be designed to change the school climate.[16] Along with changing the school environment, school officials must

9 Elbedour et al., "Cyberbullying: Roles of School Psychologists and School Counselors in Addressing a Pervasive Social Justice Issue."

10 Rosario Ortega-Ruiz and José Carlos Núñez Pérez, "Bullying and Cyberbullying: Research and Intervention at School and Social Contexts," *Psicothema*, 2012.

11 Kimberly L Mason, "Cyberbullying: A Preliminary Assessment for School Personnel," *Psychology in the Schools* 45, no. 4 (2008): 323–48; Von Marées and Petermann, "Cyberbullying: An Increasing Challenge for Schools."

12 Mason, "Cyberbullying: A Preliminary Assessment for School Personnel."

13 Kate Simmons and Yvette Bynum, "Cyberbullying: Six Things Administrators Can Do," *Education* 134, no. 4 (2014): 452–56.

14 Magdalena Marczak and Iain Coyne, "Cyberbullying at School: Good Practice and Legal Aspects in the United Kingdom," *Journal of Psychologists and Counsellors in Schools* 20, no. 2 (2010): 182–93.

15 Mason, "Cyberbullying: A Preliminary Assessment for School Personnel."

16 Elizabeth Hutson, Stephanie Kelly, and Lisa K Militello, "Systematic Review of Cyberbullying Interventions for Youth and Parents with Implications for Evidence-based Practice," *Worldviews on Evidence-based Nursing* 15, no. 1 (2018): 72–79.

have the resources available to implement prevention and intervention programs.[17]

***

With inconsiderate school interventions in cyberbullying, important legal implications are worth noting in the present analytical context. When similar interventions are perceived as a violation of student rights, there is the risk of legal issues and the potential for lawsuits.[18] It is supposable that the courts would disagree with school actions taken outside the jurisprudence (that is, past court rulings).

Sometimes there may not be a right course of action. School interventions could lead to a wide variety of problems, many of which could be outside the control of school administrators. However, it is always important for schools to define cyberbullying and plan their cyberbullying prevention program.[19]

It is undeniable that school interventions can be unnecessarily contentious; they can become a complicated affair.[20] Responses to the actions of a school administrator can be equally unpredictable.

---

[17] Charles E Notar, Sharon Padgett, and Jessica Roden, "Cyberbullying: Resources for Intervention and Prevention.," *Universal Journal of Educational Research* 1, no. 3 (2013): 133–45.

[18] Terry Diamanduros, Elizabeth Downs, and Stephen J Jenkins, "The Role of School Psychologists in the Assessment, Prevention, and Intervention of Cyberbullying," *Psychology in the Schools* 45, no. 8 (2008): 693–704.

[19] Notar, Padgett, and Roden, "Cyberbullying: Resources for Intervention and Prevention."

[20] Diamanduros, Downs, and Jenkins, "The Role of School Psychologists in the Assessment, Prevention, and Intervention of Cyberbullying."

Then again, what might explain this reality? There is no definite way to answer this question. That being said, we could examine the schools themselves to produce an acceptable explanation.

Are school officials doing everything the right way? Do school districts have the right policy documents in place? If so, do school officials regularly follow their own policy recommendations before intervening in an online incident? Currently, the answers are murky. But the debate can be fierce. Likewise, answers can be mitigated.

Critics might claim that school officials do not have clear guidance on how to address online bullying. Would there be any truth to this assertion? The answer would (probably) be yes. It is also worth noting that the cause of the problem can be misdirected. Most observers see courts as the sole culprits for school interventions. However, an alternative explanation is worthy of note. Let us explore further.

12

DEFICIENCY OF POLICY GUIDELINES

The argument could be made that the absence of clear policy procedures is the reason school officials cannot address online bullying in schools. Most school districts do not have the right policy in place. They could not properly address this issue. The problem of school intervention is unsettled. There is a bit of confusion about how school officials could deal with situations related to online misconduct.

The ineffectiveness of school officials in addressing cyberbullying can lead to fundamental questions. Observers may wonder whether school districts have the right policies in place. To address these concerns, this analysis refers to a study that explored this question.[1] These finds were shocking, although one could hardly consider them definitive. Scholars are still debating the issues.

There is no consensus in the literature, which could help explain the nature of the problem. With school interventions, the debate is growing. It is also worth outlining that the reason schools are made out to be incapable of dealing with online incidents is the extent of the conversation about school policy that deals specifically with cyberbullying. However, little is known about cyberbullying policies. The literature is laden with mistaken assumptions.

***

While school interventions in student's online conduct, which may have transpired on school grounds, can be contentious, the degree to which the courts are to blame is not settled in the debate. The belief that the courts should be blamed for school inertia on issues related to online bullying is misguided. True, there might be a few legal impediments for school officials to intervene in similar incidents. But this might be because school authorities do not have the right policy recommendations in effect to guide their intervention. To that extent, if there were an intervention crisis in cyberbullying, it would be because of a shortage of clear policies addressing the problem.

---

[1] Benjamin W. Johnson, "Cyber-Bullying Policies In K-12 Public Education: An Analysis of the Legal Implications of School Interventions" (Dissertation, University Park, Pennsylvania State University, 2012), https://etda.libraries.psu.edu/catalog/15191.

School interventions taken hoping to discipline students for a conduct, which took place off school grounds and did not [substantially] disrupt to school operations, might become problematic for both the school and staff members. While many school districts have some sets of policies in effect, the degree to which said documents were carefully designed to address online incidents remains unclear. In most cases, school officials have no clear guidance to address online issues.

The widespread belief is that public schools have the right policies in effect. But the evidence points to the contrary. For many observers, courts are prone to address the problem of school intervention poorly. They made it possible for students to misbehave online with impunity.

Notwithstanding the previous claims, a reality is irrefutable. Not every school has the right policy documents to intervene in online incidents. As a result, the deficiency of clear school policies can be at the roots of the problem in school interventions. Existing policy documents, as it may seem, are inadequate. Their enforcement can be excessively simplistic. Therefore, their effects can be too broad in scope, which could lead to legal disputes.

13

A BROAD POLICY APPROACH

Existing school policies are specifically designed to address a wide-ranging category of online misconduct by students or school staff members. These policies include incidents that took place on school grounds. They may also include off-campus behaviors. However, they may offer little or no administrative guidance to deal with fundamental constitutional ramifications, such as freedom of speech, search and seizure, and other issues, which students regularly assert in courts.

The speculation is that school districts have the proper rules, which addressed online bullying. Put differently, many believe that schools have a code of conduct in effect, which could curb student behavior whether they occurred on the Internet or elsewhere. The theory is that these tools should help school administrators reprimand student behavior on and off school grounds.

The question worth asking is how effective these strategies are. The answer might be obvious. Here, it might not be effective at all. Despite the threat of punishments, students always misbehave on the Internet. Henceforth, a narrower approach is needed in the debate.

The likelihood of legal disputes can be greater for schools that are devoid of intervention guidance than schools that have specific rules in place. Where policies are inadequate or are lacking in substance, school administrators often rely on impulses and emotions to intervene. But this is not always a clever idea.

* * *

Study shows that most policy documents addressing online bullying are misguided. While similar policies are in effect in various school districts across the United States, they do not, as a matter of fact, address many online issues, including off-campus behaviors. Accordingly, school interventions in similar incidents can be a daunting experience for school staff. Such initiatives may pose a fundamental challenge for school administrators.

Considering the contentious nature of school interventions in incidents, which could be categorized as cyberbullying, a well-advised mindset for school authorities is to understand the need to proceed with caution. It is always best for school officials to intervene with care when dealing with an online incident, especially when there are reasons to believe that the incident occurred off school grounds and no criminal law had been violated. Failing to consider these nuances could have incommensurable consequences for the school or even for the administrator involved.

It is not clear whether existing rules could help address cyberbullying problems. It is uncertain whether existing policy documents could help school leaders address incidents that occurred outside school campus.[1] A case in point may include incidents that occurred at home or off school grounds. For most observers, schools are doing everything they can to fix the problem. Rather, the courts are in the way. Is there any truth to this claim? Let us examine the nature of the debate. Let us make sense of it all.

---

[1] In an effective manner, I might add.

PART FOUR: THE REALITY OF SCHOOL POLICIES

Keywords: School districts, policy documents, school officials, literature gaps, courts, legal disputes, vague policies, disciplinary actions, legal scholars, and cyberbullying laws.

14

POPULAR ASSUMPTIONS ABOUT SCHOOL POLICIES

It is widely understood that school districts have solid policies in place to address cyberbullying. Existing policy documents could discourage students from engaging in online misdeeds. Such policies could effectively address online incidents.

Could we say that school officials always have the means and experience to address online bullying? Could we even say that school interventions are always guided by sound policy recommendations? The answers might surprise you. Here is why.

In 2012, I conducted a survey on policies that address school interventions in cyberbullying. Despite popular postulations, the debate is not resolved. Most school districts are assumed to have the policies in place to address electronic bullying. My findings suggested the opposite reality. They contradicted the notion that school policies can be effective in curbing online incidents.

The notion that schools have the right policies is wrong. This is inconceivably to be the case. It is possible that, in certain cases, school officials might have some specific strategies (or even techniques) which had helped them deal with unruly students. However, it is not clear to what extent such policies could help school officials tackle online bullying.

***

There are effective policies out there. But I would not generalize my finds. School officials are more favorable to have the right tools or correct policies to address the different online schemes, which students often used to harass or bully each other.

The mentioned study revealed that existing school policies result from unwise conventions about the role schools should play in tackling online bullying. These approaches can be based on mistaken assumptions. They are more inclined to undermine the degree to which school officials know how to discipline students for online misdeeds.

Most of the online misconduct of students occurred not on school grounds. Even when the incident occurred on campus, it did not cause a substantial disruption to school operations. Here, an important facet of the problem of bullying can be obvious.

Existing school policies on electronic bullying can be

problematic. They may exacerbate the problem for school officials. Such policies, at least from that angle alone, can be based on erroneous assumptions about school authority to police student speech outside the standards established by the courts over the years.

Certainly, schools have to authority to restrict student speech. Suggesting otherwise is misguided. In Hazelwood v. Kuhlmeier (1988), the Supreme Court held that the First Amendment rights of student journalists are not violated when school officials prevent the publication of certain articles in the school newspaper.[1] Here, schools can put a cap on student speech, which shows that school policies, when properly crafted, could make a significance in a court of law. Here, the understanding is that public schools do not have to allow students to engage in speech that is inconsistent with the schools' educational mission.

---

[1] Hazelwood School Dist. v. Kuhlmeier, 484 US 260 (Supreme Court 1988).

15

MISGUIDED POLICIES

It is irrefutable that most school districts have policies in place designed to discipline students. Unfortunately, existing policies are often based on mistaken expectations about the attitudes the court might have towards a school's disciplinary strategies. School officials often misread the intentions of courts by examining their own approach to their disciplinary roles in online matters.

Without the right policy document in place, students and parents are quick to take legal actions against the school. Thus, the problem of intervention, if we could refer to it in such a manner, does not stem from court decisions alone. Rather, it might be equated to an absence of policy recommendations to intervene [adequately] in online bullying.

When students misbehave on the Internet, school officials assess harsh punishments for the student involved. But such interventions are always contentious. Mistaken policy recommendations often attract criticism. They are also probable to cause legal disputes. This is the nature of cyber-related interventions in the United States.

***

Based on the study discussed earlier, the argument could be made that existing policy guidelines do not (specifically) address cyberbullying. The mentioned survey showed that most school policy documents are vague. Some of these policies include contradictory languages and other forms of poorly advised school intervention recommendations.

These documents include strategies that have addressed traditional bullying (or face-to-face bullying). But in similar policies, the recommendations for disciplinary actions are ambiguous. These documents often lead to misinterpretations about the intent of the courts. As a result, these misguided policy recommendations often lead to hasty (if not ill-conceived) disciplinary actions, which do not always yield positive results for school officials.

The policy recommendations uncovered during the previously reported inquiry did not address specifically online bullying; at least, they did not do so directly. Instead, these documents addressed campus actions. Other recommendations addressed common online incidents, which may not be categorized as bullying. These happenings include student behaviors, which may or may not have originated on the Internet. School interventions may occur even when there were no definite interactions among students.

Often, the victim was not aware of the conduct. On other occasions, the alleged perpetrator did not intend to the conduct to be blatant. For instance, a student who created a comment online referencing a school district or a school staff member could be treated as bullying. Regardless, schools are of a mind to take disciplinary actions against the student(s) involved under the guide of online harassment. In similar cases, parents or students are highly likely to sue the school or the officials involved.

Existing policy recommendations are not the answer to solving problems related to school interventions in cyberbullying. Policy documents have the potential to worsen the problem. School districts (that is, school professionals) often address online incidents based on impulses or instincts. This is also a perfect recipe for legal disputes, which is the foundation of the strife many observers have expressed toward the courts.

16

GAPS IN THE LITERATURE

It is important to outline obvious gaps, which pervade the literature on cyberbullying. When considering schooling in the United States, not much is known about school disciplinary actions. Most observers know little about the effects of disciplinary recommendations.

Few people outside a school setting understand why a school official might intervene in online incidents. Relying on assumptions when intervening in online issues might not be an excellent strategy. School officials may also be reluctant to intervene. For example, school officials may not intervene in an online incident if the facts are not clear. But not much is known about reluctant interventions. Fewer studies have evaluated the potential links between inadequate policies and disciplinary actions in online bullying.

On the legal front, little is known about disciplinary actions. Legal scholars often analyze cyber-related issues by referencing complex jargons, otherwise known as legalese. But that strategy is rarely useful. It cannot have a significant impact in the conversation about online bullying. It cannot clarify the problem of school interventions in similar incidents. Despite countless publications on cyberbullying, including debates on school interventions on similar issues, the nature of the intervention crisis, at least from a legal perspective, remains unclear.

***

The courts have played a key role in the establishment of cyberbullying laws. In 2010, most states, including US territories, had some laws or some status in effect, which address cyberbullying or student harassment.[1] However, the consensus is unanimous. Many see the courts as a hindrance. Despite existing policies, most school interventions ineluctably lead to unnecessary disciplinary actions.

Undeniably, school interventions based on policy guidelines, which have not been specifically designed to address online bullying, are presumable to cause many problems. For example,

---

[1] Susan Frederick and Jennifer Arguinzoni, "Cyberbullying and the States," July 9, 2010, http://www.ncsl.org/research/civil-and-criminal-justice/cyberbullying-and-the-states.aspx.

such actions are within the realm of possibility to create legal disputes. It is also worth noting that few critics would support the courts in their approach. Many observers have often criticized the courts for opinions, which some view as legally and administratively harmful to school officials.

For others, courts have proven to be an obstacle for school professionals in addressing the rise of online bullying. Many believe that court decisions have encouraged students and parents. They are bent on taking legal action against schools. This new trend has also made it impossible for school officials to intervene in cyberbullying safely and efficiently. Of course, this understanding is absurd. As will be obvious in later chapters, courts have often relied on specific legal standards to decide in cases related to school interventions in cyberbullying. It is important to make sense of the policy dilemma, which characterizes school interventions in online bullying.

Considering the issues discussed earlier, could we say, at least with a bit of certainty, that most school districts have acceptable policies in place? The answer, to reiterate, is no. The study mentioned above explored the policies of twenty-three school districts in fifteen states in the United States. The study used a content analysis method that included a mixed approach (legal analysis and qualitative analysis). You can find the study by clicking on this link (Penn State Libraries).[2]

---

[2] https://etda.libraries.psu.edu/catalog/15191

***

The findings showed that most schools did not have specific policies to address cyberbullying. Of the school districts surveyed, only one entity had specific policy documents, which offer school administrators the guideline to address online misconduct. This reality does not mean that the other schools did not have any relevant policy documents in effect. The study found other forms of policy recommendations in effect. The problem is that such policies reference student online misconduct haphazardly.

The findings suggest that most school districts have weak policies in place. These recommendations are ineffective, as they only address traditional bullying. Similar policies include the term online misconduct in their language. But they offered little or no guidance to school officials on how to avoid administrative (or even legal) effects when intervening in an incident that occurred off school grounds.

Several existing policy manuals offer little to no guidance to school professionals in taking the right initiatives. These policies are ineffective. Put differently, they cannot help school leaders curb the rise of misdeeds committed by students on the Internet.

Most policy recommendations that are in effects in schools, I would argue, are vague. They provide little or no legal reference to school officials to intervene safely and successfully in incidents that occurred online. These policies are not administratively relevant. They may have little or no legal effect. There lies the fundamental drawback in examining existing school policies on cyberbullying.

The absence of clear policy guidelines can force school administrators to intervene in online incidents by relying on impulses instead of relying on fixed recommendations, which had been expressed in several courts opinions, including landmark cases. This could be problematic. Therefore, the nature of online bullying interventions is closely tied to the policies that school districts have in place.

PART FIVE: EXAMINING COURT DECISIONS

Keywords: Types of policies, disciplinary actions, surveys, policy recommendations, the courts, legal precedents, standards, and landmark cases.

17

UNDERSTANDING THE ROLE OF THE COURTS

For many years now, the debate has been growing. It is a one-sided examination of the role that courts have played in exacerbating the online bullying intervention crisis in the United States. The prevalent belief is that courts are ambivalent in their positions.

One could argue that courts have regularly expressed their position on school interventions. Courts have often outlined how and why school officials should intervene when students engage in questionable behavior. We could make a similar argument when the conduct occurred on school grounds or in cyberspace.

To make it abundantly clear in the present context, most schools do not have the right policy documents in place. This paucity of guidance, if true, would epitomize the problem of school intervention. This reality is not necessarily a major point of friction in current discussions about school interventions in cyberbullying.

Observers are prone to blame the courts. The prevalent belief is that recent court opinions are ambiguous. The question is: how have critics been able to support that argument when the facts to the contrary are so clear?

Many observers believe that the courts have been on the side of student plaintiffs. Another point of dispute is that the courts do not provide school officials with clear guidance on how to address online issues. As a result, school leaders do not know how to respond to similar incidents. Is this the case? The answer is more complex than you may think.

***

In recent years, the courts have leaned favorably toward protecting student rights. Judiciary opinions often sided with students in disputes involving free speech claims. Although the line between online speech and online bullying can be blurry. But the wedge between traditional bullying and online misconduct can be hard to see. The courts rarely outline this difference.

The views that often criticize court rulings on issues related to school interventions in cyberbullying. Regardless of how one feels about the current debate, school officials still have a duty to address any form of student misconduct. They must do so regardless. They may intervene even though the conduct did not occur on school grounds. A caution is worth pointing out as we move forward in this analysis.

School interventions must be based on sound policies. By sound policies, the inference here includes policy recommendations that reflect jurisprudence. For school officials to intervene safely and effectively in similar incidents, they must rely on the right legal tools. These tools must include sensible policy documents. School administrators must be practical in their approach to online bullying.

***

By implementing disciplinary measures, school officials must understand the implications of their actions. Likewise, they must consider the implications of their omissions. They must also understand that online bullying is not like face-to-face bullying.

School officials should address online incidents with caution. Else, they should do so on a case-by-case basis. They should never lump incidents into the same basket, which are related to traditional bullying and online events. They should not treat every incident, including known bullying characteristics, as cyberbullying. School officials must address these instances separately and based on different rules.

It is important that school districts have specific policies in place. Such policies must unequivocally help officials address bullying in the most effective way. Policy recommendations must help officials deal with bullying in any way that is legally and administratively safe. School actions must be effective. School interventions must consider whether the incident occurred on school grounds or on the Internet.

18

LEGAL IMPLICATIONS

A s outlined at the outset of this document, online bullying is a major problem facing many schools around the world. The same is true for school districts in the United States. But the act of bullying itself cannot be ignored.[1] By that logic, school officials have a duty to address online bullying. Hesitation is never an option when students misbehave either on school grounds or elsewhere (for example, online). Hinduja and Patching (2015, p. 3) note that school personnel have "a responsibility to stop anything that has

---

[1] Sameer Hinduja and Justin W. Patchin, "Cyberbullying Legislation and Case Law: Implications for School Policy and Practic" (Cyberbullying Research Center, January 2015), https://cyberbullying.org/cyberbullying-legal-issues.pdf.

the potential to deny a student a safe learning experience."

While most states have enacted laws that address online bullying over the years, not every school has a policy manual, which specifically addresses the phenomenon at its core. Most school officials in the United States do not have the right policy tools in effect to deal with online bullying or cyber harassment. That is why this occurrence continues to wreak havoc in most American schools.

Despite many research initiatives seeking to decipher the nature of bullying, the roots cause of the problem remains murky. Not much is known about the extent of the *so-called* intervention crisis in cyberbullying. Not much is known about the crux of the issues.

The common belief is that school policies are in a perfect state. However, this is not necessarily the case. As articulated in previous chapters, it is also believed that courts are the problem. Again, this is not the case at all. In fact, in most cases, only the opposite is true.

***

Presently, bullying prevention laws are in effect in most states across the United States. As of 2015, forty-nine states (except for Montana) had adopted policies that specifically address bullying.[2] As of 2021, forty-eight states had enacted bullying prevention laws, which specifically mentioned cyberbullying or electronic harassment.[3]

---

[2] Ibid.

[3] Sameer Hinduja and Justin W. Patchin, "State Bullying Laws," Cyberbullying Research Center, 2022, https://cyberbullying.org/pdfs/2021_Bullying-and-

The popular contention is that courts are ambiguous about how school officials should proceed with online bullying incidents. This assumption, if true, would almost deny the notion that school policies are flawless. The undeniable reality is that school policy documents seldom reflect the language in existing laws. There is always room for misinterpretations, which often leads to legal disputes. But it should not be that way.

Within the context of legal precedents, state laws always reflect the language stipulated in past court decisions. Similarly, courts always refer to jurisprudence (or past rulings) to decide in cases involving freedom of speech or other pertinent constitutional issues. Thus, school policy manuals that reflect existing court decisions should pose no problem for school administrators. Sadly, the reality is seldom that obvious. The right course of actions for school officials is rarely based on a clear-cut understanding of how they should intervene.

Even though schools might have the authority to intervene in off-campus incidents, which does not presuppose that they enjoy a universal authority to act whenever they see fit. Hinduja and Patching (2015) note that school authority in online interventions is not universal. As articulated in anterior sections, school interventions must be guided by an attempt to rectify a material disruption of school operations. Short of that reality, school officials

---

Cyberbullying-Laws.pdf; Sameer Hinduja and Justin W. Patchin, "Bullying Laws and Cyberbullying Laws Across America," *Cyberbullying Research Center* (blog), 2022, https://cyberbullying.org/bullying-laws.

must be careful of their footsteps (so to speak) when they intervene in off-campus incidents.

***

The serious nature of online bullying could not be undermined. This occurrence has become a major problem in many school districts in recent years. School officials must intervene. They must protect students at all costs.

As explained in previous chapters, cyberbullying is real. It is understood as the use of electronic communication to bully a person. This typically occurs when someone sends messages to others, which intimidated or threaten them. Cyberbullying is a growing problem, not only among children but also among adolescents. Teens are vulnerable to online harassment. They are often victimized on the Internet.

Considering that cyberbullying can have profound consequences for its victims, it is always important for school officials to intervene. The legal implications of not intervening can be incommensurable. The health implications for the student being victimized by cyberbullies can be irreversible.

Online bullying can lead to anxiety, depression, and even suicide. Hence, to protect their students, school officials must intervene when they realize cyberbullying. They must do so regardless of the place of the incident.

19

THE COURTS AND CYBERBULLYING

The courts see cyberbullying as a fundamental problem. Similar incidents have been increasing in recent years. However, school districts have been struggling to come up with the best way to address the issue. Some states have passed laws that hold schools responsible for intervening in cyberbullying.

The courts have had to weigh in on several cases involving cyberbullying. In most cases, the courts have sided with the schools. They have upheld the responsibility of school officials to intervene in similar incidents. But court decisions have not been to the detriment of school interventions. Instead, the courts' position could not have been clearer. They have certainly led to many changes in how school officials deal with cyberbullying.

In consideration of recent court opinions, most schools have adopted policies, which embrace cyberbullying as a separate phenomenon in relation to traditional bullying. Presently, many schools have policies in place, which had been designed to incite prompt interventions. Such policy manuals often require school personnel to act when they realize cyberbullying.

***

The impact of court opinions and the rise of school policies could not be undermined. Such initiatives have led, some could make the case, to more effective interventions. They have also led to a decrease in incidents related to cyberbullying. This reality is incompatible with the presumption that school officials are lost; thus, could not act in online bullying.

If there were any incongruities in the role courts might have played in worsening online bullying, the facts would be irrefutable. To determine the role courts have played in setting online bulling interventions, we could examine the way courts have managed disputes related to school disciplinary actions. We could reference the jurisprudence on this issue.

An effective way to confirm the impetus of the courts in online bullying adjudications is to examine the court's position on how school officials should approach unruly students. We could reference court decisions all the way to the late 1960s. We could reference a few landmark cases in which the Supreme Court set the standard for school intervention on the matter.

***

Landmark cases, such as Tinker, Fraser, T. L. O., and others, laid the groundwork for the courts to decide in legal disputes related to freedom of speech and search and seizures. These cases are routinely cited as gold standards for other courts (at the lower level) to decide when they face similar adjudication problems. The mentioned cases make up, some might say, the irrefutable legal standards for school interventions in online-related disputes.

In Tinker v. Des Moines (1969), the Supreme Court debated whether the First Amendment protects students from speeches guaranteed by the US Constitution. The Court deliberated whether the wearing of armbands in public schools is symbolic protest, which prohibition also violates the freedom of speech of students.[1] The Court clarified that students could express themselves without material and substantial disruption.[2] Making or sharing comments with other students can fall under the first amendments of the Constitution. Making or sharing comments about school staff should not call for harsh discipline actions. Doing so would make up a blatant violation of student rights.

In Bethel School District v. Fraser (1986), the Court examined whether the First Amendment applies to public school settings. The Court debated the degree to which the First Amendment could prevent a school district from punishing a student for a speech

---

[1] Tinker v. Des Moines Independent Community School Dist., 393 US.

[2] Ibid.

deemed lewd during a school assembly.[3] The Court held that free speech rights of students differ from those of adults.[4] To clarify, that does not mean students have no rights at all. Instead, school officials must consider this reality before assessing harsh punishments to students.

In New Jersey v. T.L.O. (1985), the Supreme Court examined whether the exclusionary rule applied to search and seizure.[5] The Court debated the extent to which the Fourth Amendment applies to public schools.[6] Here, the Court held that the search for students must be reasonable.[7] Comparable searches may include electronic communications or electronic gadgets for a student, such as a computer, a phone, or a tablet. But such searches must be reasonable at the beginning.

***

Courts have used the noted gold standards in the past to decide on cases related to student behavior on school grounds and elsewhere. They have done so on various issues. They have used a similar approach in online incidents, including hazing, harassment, bullying, and search and seizure of electronic devices (for example, phones and computers).

The courts have used a similar strategy to decide on student

---

3 Bethel School Dist. No. 403 v. Fraser, 478 US 675 (Supreme Court 1986).

4 Ibid.

5 New Jersey v. TLO, 469 US 325 (Supreme Court 1985).

6 Ibid.

7 Ibid.

behaviors that are disruptive. They have regularly invoked the same standards. School officials, as is assumed in the present context, must have known these precedents. What might be at the roots of the problem then?

If school districts had policies that reflected the standards evoked in the previous paragraphs, why would intervention on these issues be controversial? Why would the courts decide against school officials? Are there valid reasons for parents to disagree with disciplinary actions taken by a school official? It is probable that there is more to the problem of intervention than most people would admit.

20

ASSESSING A RECENT STUDY

With school interventions, the courts do not always mince words. Court opinions often lay out (effectively) what Courts would tolerate in terms of disciplinary actions taken by school officials. Armed with this knowledge, the presumption is that school districts should design policies that consider both the legal issues and the administrative concerns outlined in previous court cases. But this is seldom the case. As evidence, we could reference the contentious nature of school interventions.

By relying on the findings from the study mentioned earlier, I would say that school policies are inadequate for addressing cyberbullying. They are routinely tailored based on vague language and foolish judicial expectations on how to intervene in similar issues. These policy documents are ineffective; they can lead to more legal disputes when school officials use them to address online-related incidents.

By intervening in online bullying incidents, school administrators should exercise caution. There is a need for a different approach. Faulty school policies are the reason cyberbullying interventions can be argumentative. It is also worth noting that some observers might claim otherwise.

According to critics, legal ambiguities are at the root of the problem. Courts are the major obstacle for schools to intervene safely and efficiently in cyberbullying. There is no need to challenge this assertion. Court rulings are usually not sympathetic to school-age litigants. However, they are to be inferred to decide in favor of students when no material disruption of school operations has been determined. School officials should take that into account when they adopt policies or when they intervene in online bullying.

The problem of school interventions in online bullying can be more complex than echoing the previous realities. Blaming the courts might be a convenient excuse, which might have no merit beyond ill-advised speculations. Such an approach is often the result of borrowing intents from the courts.

***

School interventions in cyberbullying are controversial because there is a scantiness of specific policy guidelines on this issue. As I tried to explain, throughout this work, most school districts do not have clear policies that address online bullying at its core. It is not surprising that school interventions in similar issues are likely to generate strong (emotional) responses from parents and students.

There is more to the problem of school intervention than most people realize. Addressing the presumed intervention predicament by evoking a mere rarity of policy guidelines is not enough. Shifting the blame may also not be enough. Although some consider the courts to be a barrier for school administrators, I see a scarcity of sound school policies as a major factor in worsening the problem. We must reconsider the reality of existing school policies.

The courts are on the right track. Their approach to school interventions is worthy. School districts must adopt new policies. They must adopt policies designed to address online incidents. School administrators must reconsider their current policy strategies. They must re-evaluate their intervention techniques. This is the best way to reduce legal complications in school interventions incidents. This is also the best way to discourage students from misbehaving on the Internet.

AFTERWORD

THERE IS A NEED FOR A NOVEL APPROACH in the debate. This book was concocted to offer such an alternative viewpoint. As we wrap up this short compilation, the question remains the same. What is the nature of online bullying interventions? Most observers do not have an answer. Although this work does not offer a definitive answer, it sought to outline the nature of the problem.

By echoing experts' analysis, the book relayed a survey that found enough evidence to support the theory that school officials are to blame on this issue of school intervention in online bullying. It may be true that with online interventions, school administrators work in the dark. But this plausibility is absurd, given the results of existing court decisions, which are unequivocal on the matter. It may not be the case that the courts deserve any blame, considering the jurisprudence. However, issues related to school interventions are more complex than most observers realize or will admit.

If you would like to learn more about school interventions in cyber-related incidents, I strongly recommend other works, which I completed about bullying. You may visit my official blog site *(https://www.benwoodpost.org)*, which includes a section on online bullying. These entries discuss issues related to cyberbullying and school interventions in greater details.

You may refer to the survey mentioned throughout the text to learn more about the extent of online bullying policies. The survey is available on the Penn State University thesis portal. You may find it here. You may also find my other work on education; they are listed at the end of the manuscript.

As you navigate the literature on school intervention in online bullying, keep in mind that school involvement can be marred by problems, some of which are foreseeable, preventable, or solvable. The courts are not ambivalent about their tolerance threshold for school interventions in cyberbullying incidents. My research shows that problems arise when school officials adopt unwise policies or when they do not follow their own policy recommendations before intervening in online incidents.

As this book sought to show, the gist of the conversation over the root cause of the problem of school interventions in cyberbullying may lie more in faulty school policies than anything else. Therefore, it is highly dubious that there is a crisis of school interventions in cyberbullying. I hope this work is persuasive enough to convince you that this is so under any plausible scenarios.

REFERENCES

Abdul-Rahim, MH. "Assessment of the Perceptions on the Effects of Cybercrime on Senior High Students in Tamale Metropolis: A Case Study of Vitting Senior High School." The University for Development Studies, 2021. http://41.66.217.101/handle/123456789/2976.

Abubey, Faith S. "County Convicts First Suspect Under Cyber Bullying Law." wfmynews2.com, February 6, 2014. https://www.wfmynews2.com/article/news/local/county -convicts-first-suspect-under-cyber-bullying-law/83- 313777058.

Ahtola, Annarilla. "Proactive and Preventive Student Welfare Activities in Finnish Preschool and Elementary School: Handling of Transition to Formal Schooling and a National Anti-Bullying Program as Examples," 2012.

Andrews, Evan. "Who Invented the Internet? - Ask History." HISTORY.com, December 18, 2013. http://www.history.com/news/ask-history/who- invented-the-internet.

Baldry, Anna Costanza, David P Farrington, and Anna Sorrentino. "'Am I at Risk of Cyberbullying'? A Narrative Review and Conceptual Framework for Research on Risk of Cyberbullying and Cybervictimization: The Risk and Needs Assessment Approach." *Aggression and Violent Behavior* 23 (2015): 36–51.

Bethel School Dist. No. 403 v. Fraser, 478 US 675 (Supreme Court 1986).

Bhat, Christine Suniti. "Cyber Bullying: Overview and Strategies for School Counsellors, Guidance Officers, and All School Personnel." *Journal of Psychologists and Counsellors in Schools* 18, no. 1 (2008): 53–66.

Brenner, Susan W. *Cybercrime: Criminal Threats from Cyberspace.* ABC-CLIO, 2010.

Broll, Ryan. "Collaborative Responses to Cyberbullying: Preventing and Responding to Cyberbullying through Nodes and Clusters." *Policing and Society* 26, no. 7 (2016): 735–52.

Butler, Des. "Cyberbullying and the Law: Parameters for Effective Interventions?" In *Reducing Cyberbullying in Schools*, 49–60. Elsevier, 2018.

Camodeca, Marina, Frits A Goossens, Mark Meerum Terwogt, and Carlo Schuengel. "Bullying and Victimization among School-age Children: Stability and Links to Proactive and Reactive Aggression." *Social Development* 11, no. 3 (2002): 332–45.

Campbell, Evelyn M, and Susan E Smalling. "American Indians and Bullying in Schools," 2013.

Cantone, Elisa, Anna P Piras, Marcello Vellante, Antonello Preti, Sigrun Daníelsdóttir, Ernesto D'Aloja, Sigita Lesinskiene, Mathhias C Angermeyer, Mauro G Carta, and Dinesh Bhugra. "Interventions on Bullying and Cyberbullying in Schools: A Systematic Review." *Clinical Practice and Epidemiology in Mental Health: CP & EMH* 11, no. Suppl 1 M4 (2015): 58.

CBS News. "Cyberbully Mom Guilty Of Lesser Charge," November 26, 2008. https://www.cbsnews.com/news/cyberbully-mom-guilty-of-lesser-charge/.

Cho, Chang-Hoan, and Hongsik John Cheon. "Children's Exposure to Negative Internet Content: Effects of Family Context." *Journal of Broadcasting & Electronic Media* 49, no. 4 (December 1, 2005): 488–509. https://doi.org/10.1207/s15506878jobem4904_8.

Conn, Kathleen. "Cyberbullying and Other Student Technology Misuses in K-12 American Schools: The Legal Landmines." *Widener L. Rev.* 16 (2010): 89.

Corliss, Cindy L. "The Established and the Outsiders: Cyberbullying as an Exclusionary Process," 2017.

Daigle, Leslie. "On the Nature of the Internet." Paper series. Global Commission on Internet Governance. The Centre for International Governance Innovation and Chatham House, March 16, 2015. https://www.cigionline.org/sites/default/files/gcig_paper_no7.pdf.

Diamanduros, Terry, Elizabeth Downs, and Stephen J Jenkins. "The Role of School Psychologists in the Assessment, Prevention, and Intervention of Cyberbullying." *Psychology in the Schools* 45, no. 8 (2008): 693–704.

Dooley, Julian J, Jacek Pyżalski, and Donna Cross. "Cyberbullying versus Face-to-Face Bullying: A Theoretical and Conceptual Review." *Zeitschrift Für Psychologie/Journal of Psychology* 217, no. 4 (2009): 182.

eBizMBA. "Top 15 Most Popular Social Networking Sites." eBizMBA, November 2022. http://www.ebizmba.com/articles/social-networking-websites.

Elbedour, Salman, Salihah Alqahtani, Ibrahim El Sheikh Rihan, Joseph A Bawalsah, Beverly Booker-Ammah, and J Fidel Turner Jr. "Cyberbullying: Roles of School Psychologists and School Counselors in Addressing a Pervasive Social

Justice Issue." *Children and Youth Services Review* 109 (2020): 104720.

Elinoff, Mahri J, Sandra M Chafouleas, and Kari A Sassu. "Bullying: Considerations for Defining and Intervening in School Settings." *Psychology in the Schools* 41, no. 8 (2004): 887–97.

Eslea, Mike, and Peter K Smith. "The Long-term Effectiveness of Anti-bullying Work in Primary Schools." *Educational Research* 40, no. 2 (1998): 203–18.

Feinberg, Ted, and Nicole Robey. "Cyberbullying: Intervention and Prevention Strategies." *National Association of School Psychologists* 38, no. 4 (2009): 22–24.

Frederick, Susan, and Jennifer Arguinzoni. "Cyberbullying and the States," July 9, 2010. http://www.ncsl.org/research/civil-and-criminal-justice/cyberbullying-and-the-states.aspx.

Gaffney, Hannah, David P Farrington, Dorothy L Espelage, and Maria M Ttofi. "Are Cyberbullying Intervention and Prevention Programs Effective? A Systematic and Meta-Analytical Review." *Aggression and Violent Behavior* 45 (2019): 134–53.

Goodno, Naomi Harlin. "How Public Schools Can Constitutionally Halt Cyberbullying: A Model Cyberbullying Policy That Considers First Amendment, Due Process, and Fourth Amendment Challenges." *Wake Forest L. Rev.* 46 (2011): 641.

Hazelwood School Dist. v. Kuhlmeier, 484 US 260 (Supreme Court 1988).

Hinduja, Sameer, and Justin W. Patchin. "Bullying Laws and Cyberbullying Laws Across America." *Cyberbullying Research Center* (blog), 2022. https://cyberbullying.org/bullying-laws.

———. "Cyberbullying Legislation and Case Law: Implications for School Policy and Practic." Cyberbullying Research Center, January 2015. https://cyberbullying.org/cyberbullying-legal-issues.pdf.

———. "State Bullying Laws." Cyberbullying Research Center, 2022. https://cyberbullying.org/pdfs/2021_Bullying-and-Cyberbullying-Laws.pdf.

Hinduja, Sameer, and Justin W Patchin. "State Cyberbullying Laws." *Cyberbullying Research Center*, 2012.

Hinduja, Sameer, and Justin W. Patchin. "Teen Sexting – A Brief Guide for Educators and Parents." Cyberbullying Research Center, 2022. https://cyberbullying.org/sexting-research-summary-2022.pdf.

Hsu, Jeremy. "Can Humans Survive?" LiveScience.com, March 7, 2022. http://www.livescience.com/9956-humans-survive.html.

Hutson, Elizabeth, Stephanie Kelly, and Lisa K Militello. "Systematic Review of Cyberbullying Interventions for Youth and Parents with Implications for Evidence-based Practice." *Worldviews on Evidence-based Nursing* 15, no. 1 (2018): 72–79.

Internet World Stats. "Internet Growth Statistics: Today's Road to e-Commerce and Global Trade Internet Technology Reports," July 31, 2022. http://www.internetworldstats.com/emarketing.htm.

James, Alana. "School Bullying." *Res Briefing Nedlastet Fra Www Nspcc Org Uk/Inform* 26 (2010): 2012.

Johnson, Benjamin W. "Cyber-Bullying Policies In K-12 Public Education: An Analysis of the Legal Implications of School Interventions." Dissertation, Pennsylvania State University, 2012. https://etda.libraries.psu.edu/catalog/15191.

Juvonen, Jaana, and Sandra Graham. "Bullying in Schools: The Power of Bullies and the Plight of Victims." *Annual Review of Psychology* 65, no. 1 (2014): 159–85.

Juvonen, Jaana, and Elisheva F Gross. "Extending the School Grounds?—Bullying Experiences in Cyberspace." *Journal of School Health* 78, no. 9 (2008): 496–505.

Kagita, Mohan Krishna, Navod Thilakarathne, Thippa Reddy Gadekallu, Praveen Kumar Reddy Maddikunta, and Saurabh Singh. "A Review on Cyber Crimes on the Internet of Things." *Deep Learning for Security and Privacy Preservation in IoT*, 2021, 83–98.

Kintonova, Aliya, Alexander Vasyaev, and Viktor Shestak. "Cyberbullying and Cyber-Mobbing in Developing Countries." *Information & Computer Security*, 2021.

Kowalski, Robin M, and Susan P Limber. "Electronic Bullying among Middle School Students." *Journal of Adolescent Health* 41, no. 6 (2007): S22–30.

Kuipers, AAL. "Real Life Social Self-Esteem Affects Children's Likelihood to Be a Victim of Cyberbullying.," 2018.

Lane, Darcy K. "Taking the Lead on Cyberbullying: Why Schools Can and Should Protect Students Online." *Iowa L. Rev.* 96 (2010): 1791.

Laucius, Joanne. "Why Some Victims Become Bullies: Q&A with Bullying Expert Tracy Vaillancourt." Ottawa Citizen, November 23, 2014. http://ottawacitizen.com/news/local-news/why-some-victims-become-bullies-qa-with-bullying-expert-tracy-vaillancourt.

Li, Qing. "Cyberbullying in Schools: A Research of Gender Differences." *School Psychology International* 27, no. 2 (2006): 157–70.

———. "New Bottle but Old Wine: A Research of Cyberbullying in Schools." *Computers in Human Behavior* 23, no. 4 (2007): 1777–91.

Lidsky, Lyrissa, and Andrea Pinzon Garcia. "How Not to Criminalize Cyberbullying." *Mo. L. Rev.* 77 (2012): 693.

Lowry, Paul Benjamin, Jun Zhang, Chuang Wang, and Mikko Siponen. "Why Do Adults Engage in Cyberbullying on Social Media? An Integration of Online Disinhibition and Deindividuation Effects with the Social Structure and

Social Learning Model." *Information Systems Research* 27, no. 4 (2016): 962–86.

Mahato, Ranjan. "History of the Internet and Popularity of the Internet." HubPages, May 22, 2013. http://hubpages.com/technology/History-of-the-Internet-and-specialty-of-the-Internet.

Marczak, Magdalena, and Iain Coyne. "Cyberbullying at School: Good Practice and Legal Aspects in the United Kingdom." *Journal of Psychologists and Counsellors in Schools* 20, no. 2 (2010): 182–93.

Mason, Kimberly L. "Cyberbullying: A Preliminary Assessment for School Personnel." *Psychology in the Schools* 45, no. 4 (2008): 323–48.

McAdams III, Charles R, and Christopher D Schmidt. "How to Help a Bully: Recommendations for Counseling the Proactive Aggressor." *Professional School Counseling* 11, no. 2 (2007): 2156759X0701100207.

Mori, Camille, Julianna Park, Jeff R. Temple, and Sheri Madigan. "Are Youth Sexting Rates Still on the Rise? A Meta-Analytic Update." *The Journal of Adolescent Health: Official Publication of the Society for Adolescent Medicine* 70, no. 4 (April 2022): 531–39. https://doi.org/10.1016/j.jadohealth.2021.10.026.

Mouheb, Djedjiga, Masa Hilal Abushamleh, Maya Hilal Abushamleh, Zaher Al Aghbari, and Ibrahim Kamel. "Real-Time Detection of Cyberbullying in Arabic Twitter Streams," 1–5. IEEE, 2019.

Myers, Carrie-Anne, and Helen Cowie. "Cyberbullying across the Lifespan of Education: Issues and Interventions from School to University." *International Journal of Environmental Research and Public Health* 16, no. 7 (2019): 1217.

Namie, Gary. "2021 WBI US Workplace Bullying Survey." *Workplace Bullying Institute* (blog), February 24, 2021. https://workplacebullying.org/2021-wbi-survey/.

Namie, Gary, and Ruth Namie. "Are You Being Bullied At Work?" *Workplace Bullying Institute* (blog), 2022. https://workplacebullying.org/.

New Jersey v. T.L.O., 469 US 325 (Supreme Court 1985).

Nilan, Pam, Haley Burgess, Mitchell Hobbs, Steven Threadgold, and Wendy Alexander. "Youth, Social Media, and Cyberbullying Among Australian Youth: 'Sick Friends.'" *Social Media + Society* 1, no. 2 (July 1, 2015): 2056305115604848. https://doi.org/10.1177/2056305115604848.

Notar, Charles E, Sharon Padgett, and Jessica Roden. "Cyberbullying: Resources for Intervention and Prevention." *Universal Journal of Educational Research* 1, no. 3 (2013): 133–45.

Ortega-Ruiz, Rosario, and José Carlos Núñez Pérez. "Bullying and Cyberbullying: Research and Intervention at School and Social Contexts." *Psicothema*, 2012.

Ovejero, Anastasio, Santiago Yubero, Elisa Larrañaga, and María de la V Moral. "Cyberbullying: Definitions and Facts from a Psychosocial Perspective." In *Cyberbullying across the Globe*, 1–31. Springer, 2016.

Patchin, Justin W. "The Status of Sexting Laws Across the United States." *Cyberbullying Research Center* (blog), August 18, 2022. https://cyberbullying.org/the-status-of-sexting-laws-across-the-united-states.

Patchin, Justin W, and Sameer Hinduja. "Bullies Move beyond the Schoolyard: A Preliminary Look at Cyberbullying." *Youth Violence and Juvenile Justice* 4, no. 2 (2006): 148–69.

———. "School-Based Efforts to Prevent Cyberbullying." *The Prevention Researcher* 19, no. 3 (2012): 7–10.

Philipson, Jon M. "Kids Are Not All Right: Mandating Peer Mediation as a Proactive Anti-Bullying Measure in Schools." *Cardozo J. Conflict Resol.* 14 (2012): 81.

Pitts, John, and Philip Smith. *Preventing School Bullying.* Citeseer, 1995.

Primack, Alvin J, and Kevin A Johnson. "Student Cyberbullying inside the Digital Schoolhouse Gate: Toward a Standard for Determining Where a 'School' Is." *First Amendment Studies* 51, no. 1 (2017): 30–48.

Rao, TS Sathyanarayana, Deepali Bansal, and Suhas Chandran. "Cyberbullying: A Virtual Offense with Real Consequences." *Indian Journal of Psychiatry* 60, no. 1 (2018): 3.

Raskauskas, Juliana, and Ann D Stoltz. "Involvement in Traditional and Electronic Bullying among Adolescents." *Developmental Psychology* 43, no. 3 (2007): 564.

Ravenscraft, Eric. "Why the FCC's New Net Neutrality Rules Are Good for the Internet." Lifehacker, February 26, 2015. http://lifehacker.com/why-the-fccs-new-net-neutrality-rules-are-good-for-the-1683769527.

Rigby, Ken. "School Perspectives on Bullying and Preventative Strategies: An Exploratory Study." *Australian Journal of Education* 61, no. 1 (2017): 24–39.

———. "What Can Schools Do about Cases of Bullying?" *Pastoral Care in Education* 29, no. 4 (2011): 273–85.

Rigby, Ken, and Kaye Johnson. *The Prevalence and Effectiveness of Anti-Bullying Strategies Employed in Australian Schools.* University of South Australia Adelaide, 2016.

Rigby, Ken, and Peter K Smith. "Is School Bullying Really on the Rise?" *Social Psychology of Education* 14, no. 4 (2011): 441–55.

Ryan, Susan Maree. "The Internet Playground: One School's Experience of Cyberbullying," 2017.

Sabella, Russell A., Justin W. Patchin, and Sameer Hinduja. "Cyberbullying Myths and Realities." *Computers in Human Behavior* 29, no. 6 (November 1, 2013): 2703–11. https://doi.org/10.1016/j.chb.2013.06.040.

Samara, Muthanna, and Peter K Smith. "How Schools Tackle Bullying, and the Use of Whole School Policies: Changes over the Last Decade." *Educational Psychology* 28, no. 6 (2008): 663–76.

Seay III, James L. "Salvaging the North Carolina Teacher-Cyberbullying Statute." *Campbell L. Rev.* 37 (2015): 391.

Sezer, Nilüfer, and Serdar Tunçer. "Cyberbullying Hurts: The Rising Threat to Youth in the Digital Age." *Digital Siege (Ss. 179-194). Istanbul: Istanbul University Press. Https://Doi. Org/10.26650/B/SS07* 9 (2021).

Shariff, Shaheen, and Dianne L Hoff. "Cyber Bullying: Clarifying Legal Boundaries for School Supervision in Cyberspace," 2016.

Simmons, Kate, and Yvette Bynum. "Cyberbullying: Six Things Administrators Can Do." *Education* 134, no. 4 (2014): 452–56.

Slonje, Robert, and Peter K Smith. "Cyberbullying: Another Main Type of Bullying?" *Scandinavian Journal of Psychology* 49, no. 2 (2008): 147–54.

Smith, Peter K, Allison Kupferberg, Joaquin A Mora-Merchan, Muthanna Samara, Sue Bosley, and Rob Osborn. "A Content Analysis of School Anti-Bullying Policies: A Follow-up after Six Years." *Educational Psychology in Practice* 28, no. 1 (2012): 47–70.

Smith, Peter K, Jess Mahdavi, Manuel Carvalho, Sonja Fisher, Shanette Russell, and Neil Tippett. "Cyberbullying: Its Nature and Impact in Secondary School Pupils." *Journal of Child Psychology and Psychiatry* 49, no. 4 (2008): 376–85.

Smith, Peter K, Cherise Smith, Rob Osborn, and Muthanna Samara. "A Content Analysis of School Anti-bullying Policies: Progress and Limitations." *Educational Psychology in Practice* 24, no. 1 (2008): 1–12.

Smith, Robert W, and Kayce Smith. "Creating the Cougar Watch: Learning to Be Proactive against Bullying in Schools. Despite Reticence from the Central Office, Strong Middle

Level Teacher Leaders Worked Together to Develop an Effective Anti-Bullying Program That Addresses a Significant Need for Safety and Inclusion for All Middle School Students." *Middle School Journal* 46, no. 1 (2014): 13–19.

Stauffer, Sterling, Melissa Allen Heath, Sarah Marie Coyne, and Scott Ferrin. "High School Teachers' Perceptions of Cyberbullying Prevention and Intervention Strategies." *Psychology in the Schools* 49, no. 4 (2012): 352–67.

Steinhauer, Jennifer. "Verdict in MySpace Suicide Case." *The New York Times*, November 26, 2008, sec. US https://www.nytimes.com/2008/11/27/us/27myspace.html.

Sticca, Fabio. "Bullying Goes Online: Definition, Risk Factors, Consequences, and Prevention of (Cyber) Bullying," 2013.

Studer, Jeannine R, and Blair S Mynatt. "Bullying Prevention in Middle Schools: A Collaborative Approach: Collaborative, Proactive Anti-Bullying Interventions and Policies That Strive to Create and Sustain a Safe Environment for All Adolescents." *Middle School Journal* 46, no. 3 (2015): 25–32.

Thompson, Fran, and Peter K Smith. "The Use and Effectiveness of Anti-Bullying Strategies in Schools." *Research Brief DFE-RR098*, 2011, 1–220.

Tinker v. Des Moines Independent Community School Dist., 393 US 503 (Supreme Court 1969).

Tokunaga, Robert S. "Following You Home from School: A Critical Review and Synthesis of Research on Cyberbullying Victimization." *Computers in Human Behavior* 26, no. 3 (2010): 277–87.

US Equal Employment Opportunity Commission. "Harassment," 2016. http://www.eeoc.gov/laws/types/harassment.cfm.

Valkenburg, Patti M., and Jochen Peter. "Social Consequences of the Internet for Adolescents A Decade of Research." *Current Directions in Psychological Science* 18, no. 1

(February 1, 2009): 1–5. https://doi.org/10.1111/j.1467-8721.2009.01595.x.

Von Marées, Nandoli, and Franz Petermann. "Cyberbullying: An Increasing Challenge for Schools." *School Psychology International* 33, no. 5 (2012): 467–76.

Waldman, Ari Ezra. "Tormented: Antigay Bullying in Schools." *Temp. L. Rev.* 84 (2011): 385.

Weinstein, Emily C., and Robert L. Selman. "Digital Stress: Adolescents' Personal Accounts." *New Media & Society* 18, no. 3 (March 1, 2016): 391–409. https://doi.org/10.1177/1461444814543989.

Weinstein, Emily C., Robert L. Selman, Sara Thomas, Jung-Eun Kim, Allison E. White, and Karthik Dinakar. "How to Cope With Digital Stress The Recommendations Adolescents Offer Their Peers Online." *Journal of Adolescent Research*, June 18, 2015, 0743558415587326. https://doi.org/10.1177/0743558415587326.

Wiederhold, Brenda K. "Cyberbullying and LGBTQ Youth: A Deadly Combination." *Cyberpsychology, Behavior, and Social Networking* 17, no. 9 (2014): 569–70.

Williams, Kirk R, and Nancy G Guerra. "Prevalence and Predictors of Internet Bullying." *Journal of Adolescent Health* 41, no. 6 (2007): S14–21.

Yang, Y Tony, and Erin Grinshteyn. "Safer Cyberspace through Legal Intervention: A Comparative Review of Cyberbullying Legislation." *World Medical & Health Policy* 8, no. 4 (2016): 458–77.

Ybarra, Michele L, and Kimberly J Mitchell. "Online Aggressor/Targets, Aggressors, and Targets: A Comparison of Associated Youth Characteristics." *Journal of Child Psychology and Psychiatry* 45, no. 7 (2004): 1308–16.

Young, Rachel, Melissa Tully, and Marizen Ramirez. "School Administrator Perceptions of Cyberbullying Facilitators

and Barriers to Preventive Action: A Qualitative Study."
Health Education & Behavior 44, no. 3 (2017): 476–84.

Zaborskis, Apolinaras, Gabriela Ilionsky, Riki Tesler, and Andreas
Heinz. "The Association between Cyberbullying, School
Bullying, and Suicidality among Adolescents: Findings
from the Cross-National Study HBSC in Israel, Lithuania,
and Luxembourg." *Crisis: The Journal of Crisis Intervention
and Suicide Prevention* 40, no. 2 (2019): 100.

Zych, Izabela, Anna C Baldry, and David P Farrington. "School
Bullying and Cyberbullying: Prevalence, Characteristics,
Outcomes, and Prevention." *Handbook of Behavioral
Criminology*, 2017, 113–38.

INDEX

A

Abolish bullying, *22, 137*
Academic, *3, 22, 137, 144*
   Academic lexicon, *3, 137*
   Academic problems, *22, 137*
Acceptable, *74, 95, 137*
Administrative, *49, 59, 66–7, 79, 96, 115, 137*
   Administrative complications, *67, 137*
   Administrative concerns, *115, 137*
   Administrative guidance, *79, 137*
   Administrative hurdles, *59, 66, 137*
Administrator (see: School)
Adolescents, *10, 15, 18, 21, 24, 28, 34–6, 44, 55–6, 60, 71, 108, 131, 133–5, 137, 142*
Adult, *7, 15, 36, 44–5, 112, 128, 137, 142, 146*
   Adult Americans, *7, 137*
Aggression, *8, 21, 24, 34, 36–7, 41, 44, 53–4, 61, 124, 126, 137, 139*
Aggressive, *57, 137*
Aggressors, *16, 36, 44, 134, 137*
Aggrieved parents (see: Lawsuits)

Amendment (see: Student Right)
   Amendment rights, *50, 87, 137*
America, *42, 107, 126, 137, 144, 146*
   American, *3, 7, 10, 17, 27, 42, 53, 56, 106, 124–5, 137, 146*
   American educators, *10, 137, 146*
   American school, *3, 27, 42, 56, 106, 125, 137*
   American youth, *17, 137*
Anti-bullying, *28, 49, 53–6, 59–60, 71, 123, 130–3, 137*
   Anti-bullying initiatives, *56, 137*
   Anti-bullying measure, *55–6, 59, 130, 137*
   Anti-bullying policy, *54–5, 60, 132, 137*
   Anti-bullying programs, *28, 56, 137*
Anti-cyberbullying (see: Anti-bullying)

B

Behavior, *8, 11–2, 15, 21, 23–4, 30, 33–4, 48, 51–2, 55, 61, 69–70, 79–80, 91, 101, 112–3, 124, 126, 128, 131, 133–5, 137, 141*
Bullied, *7, 34, 44, 130, 137*

Bully, *11–2, 15–6, 22–3, 27–30, 35, 42–4, 47, 54, 86, 108, 127–30, 137, 141*
Bullying, *1–3, 7–13, 15–6, 18–24, 27–31, 33–7, 39, 42–57, 60–1, 65–6, 70–2, 74–6, 79–80, 85–6, 90–1, 94–7, 101–3, 105–8, 110, 112, 116–7, 119–20, 123–35, 137–41*
  Case, *3, 8–9, 12, 28, 46, 48, 50, 53, 71, 77, 81, 86–7, 91, 95, 97, 99, 102, 106–7, 109–12, 115, 119, 124, 126, 130–1, 133, 137–8, 140*
    Court, *29, 50, 54, 60, 65–6, 73–4, 76–7, 79, 81, 83, 87, 89–91, 94–5, 97, 99, 101–2, 104, 106–7, 109–17, 119–20, 124, 126, 130, 133, 138–9*
      Court cases, *115, 138*
      Court decisions, *65, 89, 95, 99, 107, 109–10, 119, 138*
      Court opinions, *102, 110, 115, 138*
      Court rulings, *29, 73, 102, 116, 138*

C
Case-by-case, *103, 138*
Children (see: Young)
Communication, *22, 30, 35–6, 41, 47, 108, 112, 138*
Computer, *8, 11, 15, 45, 51, 55, 112, 128, 131, 133, 138*
  Computer crimes, *45, 138*
  Computer fraud, *8, 138*
Consensus, *3, 43, 49, 76, 94, 138*
Constitution, *60, 111, 138*
Constitutional, *50, 60, 63, 65, 79, 107, 138*
  Constitutional issues, *107, 138*
  Constitutional rights, *60, 63, 138*
  Constitutional violations, *65, 138*
Crimes, *45–6, 128, 138*
  Criminal, *45, 49, 81, 124, 138, 143–4*
  Criminality, *45–6, 138*
  Criminalize, *49, 128, 138*
  Criminalizing, *48, 138*
Criminal law, *81, 138*
  Criminal punishments, *49, 138*
Crisis (see: Intervene - Intervention)

Criticism, *25, 67, 90, 138*
Cyberbullying, *1–3, 5, 8–13, 15–9, 21–5, 27–37, 42–51, 55–7, 59–63, 65–7, 69–73, 75–7, 80–1, 83, 85, 87, 90–1, 93–7, 102–3, 105–14, 116–7, 120–1, 124–35, 138–42, 144, 146*
  Cyberbully, *8, 16, 29, 39, 46, 50–1, 108, 125, 138*
Cyber criminality, *5, 45–6, 138*
  Cybercriminals, *46, 138*
Cyber harassment, *4, 106, 138*
Cyber-related, *2, 67, 90, 94, 120, 138*
  Cyber-related incidents, *2, 120, 138*
  Cyber-related issues, *94, 138*
  Cyber-related school interventions, *67, 138*
Cyberspace, *9, 11–2, 16, 22–3, 29–30, 35–7, 42–3, 45, 50–1, 101, 124, 127, 132, 134, 138*

D
Deaths, *29, 138*
Debate, *30, 43, 48, 52, 54, 61, 67, 70, 74, 76, 80–1, 86, 94, 101–2, 119, 138*
Decisions, *65, 89, 95, 99, 107, 109–10, 119, 138*
  Supreme court (see: Bullying - Case)
Demoralizing, *9, 45, 138*
Depressing, *9, 138*
Depression, *23, 108, 138*
Depressive (symptoms), *69, 138*
Deterrence, *48, 138*
Disciplinary, *5, 46, 49, 51–2, 66, 71, 83, 89–91, 93–4, 99, 103, 110, 113, 115, 138, 140*
Discipline, *77, 86, 89, 111, 138*
Disgruntled, *52, 138*
Disproportionate, *71, 138*
Dispute, *19, 67, 77, 80, 83, 90–1, 95, 102, 107, 110–1, 116, 138*
Disrupt, *77, 138, 141*
  Disruption, *66, 77, 86, 107, 111, 116, 138, 141*
  Disruptive, *60–1, 113, 138*
Distress, *18, 21, 23, 138*
District, *18–9, 27–30, 50, 54, 61–2, 70, 74–5, 77, 79–80, 83, 85–6, 89, 91,*

95–7, 103, 105, 108–9, 111, 113, 115, 117, 138, 140

E

Education, 15–6, 18, 20, 28, 31, 48, 62, 71–2, 76, 120, 127, 129, 131–2, 135, 138, 144, 146

Educational, 16, 54–5, 73, 87, 126, 130, 132, 138, 144

Educators, 10, 12, 127, 137–8, 146

Egregious, 49, 138

Electronic, 3, 10–1, 16, 21, 23–4, 28, 30, 34–5, 44, 46–8, 50, 86, 106, 108, 112, 125, 128, 131, 138

Elementary, 15–6, 18, 20, 56, 123, 138

E-mail, 22, 138, 144

Emotions, 59, 80, 138

Enforcement, 77, 138, 143

Ethical, 67, 138

Evidence, 72, 77, 115, 119, 127, 138

Expressed, 91, 97, 101, 138

Expressing, 42, 138

Expression, 50, 138, 141

Expulsion, 49, 139, 141

F

Facebook (see: Social)

Face-to-face, 9–11, 21, 23–4, 28–30, 34, 42, 44, 90, 103, 125, 139

    Traditional bullying, 10

  Face-to-face aggressions, 34, 139

  Face-to-face bullying, 21, 23, 28–30, 34, 90, 103, 125, 139

  Face-to-face harassment, 11, 28, 34, 139

  Face-to-face misconduct, 24, 139

Faulty, 116, 120, 139

Felony conviction, 8, 139

G

Gadgets, 11, 112, 139

Gender, 2, 12–3, 29, 34, 45, 128, 139

Generalize, 86, 139

Girl, 42, 139

Goal, 48, 139

Gold, 111–2, 139

Guidance, 55, 65, 74, 77, 79–80, 96, 102, 124, 137, 139

Guidelines, 55–6, 63, 75–6, 78, 90, 94, 97, 116–7, 139

Guilty, 8–9, 125, 139

H

Harass, 9, 12, 23, 41, 43, 86, 139

Harassing, 18, 139

Harassment, 2, 4, 8–12, 15, 24, 28, 34, 42, 44–5, 55, 91, 94, 106, 108, 112, 133, 138–9, 141

Harmful, 22, 95, 139

Hazelwood, 87, 126, 139

Hostile, 54, 139

I

Impersonating, 8, 139

Impulses, 80, 91, 97, 139

Impulsions, 59, 139

Impulsive, 50, 139

Impunity, 35, 77, 139

Inconsistent, 3, 87, 139

Inconsistent approaches (see: School - Policy)

Injustice, 54, 139

In-person, 10, 139

Insults, 2, 29, 50, 139

Internet, 1–3, 8–12, 15–9, 29, 33–7, 41, 43–8, 60, 66, 80, 90–1, 96, 104, 108, 117, 123, 125, 127–9, 131, 133–4, 139

  Internet-based, 45, 139

  Internet-related, 16–7, 19, 42, 139

Intervene, 28, 43, 60–2, 67, 70–1, 76–7, 80, 89, 93, 95–7, 101–3, 107–9, 116, 139, 141

Intervening, 34, 54, 57, 67, 74, 93, 96, 108–9, 116, 120, 126, 139

Intervention, 3, 5, 10, 19, 24, 29–30, 39, 50–63, 65–7, 69–77, 80, 85, 89–91, 94–5, 97, 101–4, 106–7, 109–11, 113, 115–7, 119–20, 124–7, 129–30, 133–5, 138–41

Intimidate, 9, 23, 108, 139

Intimidation, 2, 10, 139

Invasive, 9, 139

J

Jargons, 94, 139

Jersey, 112, 130, 139

Jokes, 2, 139

Journalists, 87, 139, 141

Judge, 2, 139

Judicial, *116, 139*
Judiciary, *102, 139*
Jurisprudence, *66, 73, 103, 107, 110, 119, 139*
    Precedents (see: Bullying - Case - Court)
Jury, *9, 139*
K
Keywords, *5, 39, 63, 83, 99, 139*
Knowledge, *70, 115, 139*
Kuhlmeier, *87, 126, 139*
L
Label, *52, 139*
Labeled, *10, 139*
Lack, *21–2, 24, 26, 52, 62, 139*
Lacking, *80, 139*
Landmark, *8, 97, 99, 110–1, 139*
Laws, *2, 12, 83, 94, 106–7, 109, 126–7, 130, 133, 139*
Lawsuits, *29, 51, 66, 70, 73, 137, 139*
Leadership, *71, 139, 144, 146*
Legal, *5, 9, 19, 29, 50–2, 56, 59, 62, 67, 72–3, 76–7, 80, 83, 89–91, 94–6, 99, 103, 105–8, 111, 115–7, 125, 127, 129, 132, 134, 139, 144–5*
Legalese, *94, 139*
Legally, *37, 95, 103, 140*
Literature, *3, 10, 19, 28–30, 34, 43, 76, 83, 93–4, 96, 98, 120, 140*
Litigants, *116, 140*
Litigation, *54, 67, 140*
M
Male, *12, 29, 45, 140*
Manual, *96, 106–7, 110, 140*
Mediation, *55–6, 59, 130, 140*
Messages, *12, 22–3, 108, 140*
Messaging, *22–3, 140*
Middle, *11–2, 23, 34–5, 55–6, 60, 128, 132–3, 140*
Misbehave, *33, 37, 43, 67, 70, 77, 80, 90, 105, 140*
Misbehaving, *33–4, 36, 38, 117, 140*
Misconceptions, *70*
Misconduct, *3, 9, 11, 19, 22, 24, 29, 42, 46, 49, 51, 75, 79, 86, 96, 102, 139–41*
Misdeeds, *3, 24, 85–6, 96, 140*

Misdemeanor, *8, 140*
Misgivings, *41, 140*
Misinterpretations, *90, 107, 140*
MySpace, *8–9, 133, 140*
N
Name-calling, *29, 140*
Network, *1, 36, 140*
O
Occurrence, *3, 8–9, 11–2, 16, 22, 27, 29–30, 33, 106, 108, 140*
Outlaw, *49, 140*
P
Peer-to-peer, *18, 140*
Psyche, *23–4, 140*
Psychological, *18, 21, 23, 72, 133, 140*
Psychosocial, *22–3, 36, 66, 130, 140*
Punish, *43, 48, 50–1*
Punished, *60, 140*
Punishing, *111, 140*
Punishment, *5, 48–50, 80, 90, 112, 138, 140*
Put-downs, *2, 140*
R
Real-life, *30, 140*
Real-world, *30, 140*
Recommendations, *18, 49, 54, 60, 74, 76, 85, 89–91, 93, 96–7, 99, 103, 120, 129, 134, 140*
Repercussions, *29, 140*
Reprimand, *80, 140*
Robert bishop (see: Bullying - Case)
Rule, *18, 49, 60, 79–81, 103, 112, 131, 140–1*
Rulings, *29, 73, 102, 107, 116, 138, 140*
S
Safe, *36, 54–6, 60, 103, 133, 140–1*
Safely, *61, 71, 95–6, 103, 116, 140*
Safety, *54–6, 133, 140–1*
Sanction, *49, 140*
School, *2–3, 5, 8, 10–3, 15–9, 22–4, 27–31, 33–5, 37, 39, 41–63, 65–7, 69–77, 79–81, 83, 85–91, 93–7, 101–13, 115–7, 119–20, 123–35, 137–41, 144*
    Parent, *2, 12, 17, 29, 48, 51–2, 71–2, 89, 91, 95, 113, 117, 127, 137, 140–1*

Policy, *3, 39, 49–56, 58, 60–3, 70, 74–83, 85–92, 94–7, 99, 102–3, 105–7, 110, 113, 115–7, 120, 126–7, 132–4, 137, 139–41, 144–6*

School actions, *24, 39, 62, 66, 71, 73, 103, 140*

School administration, *51, 63, 140*

School administrator, *2, 19, 29, 34, 48–9, 60, 67, 73, 80, 96–7, 103, 107, 116–7, 119, 140*

School-age, *15–6, 29, 34, 116, 140*

School-age children, *15–6, 29, 34, 140*

School-age litigants, *116, 140*

School assembly, *112, 140*

School authority, *50, 76, 80, 87, 107, 140*

School bullying, *31, 47–8, 53, 56, 71, 127, 131, 135, 140*

Schoolchild, *42, 140*

School climate, *72, 140*

School community, *72, 140*

School disciplinary, *93, 110, 140*

School district, *18–9, 27–30, 50, 54, 61–2, 70, 74–5, 77, 79–80, 83, 85–6, 89, 91, 95–7, 103, 105, 108–9, 111, 113, 115, 117, 140*

School grounds, *3, 16, 22–3, 29, 35, 42, 45, 51–2, 60, 76–7, 79–81, 86, 96, 101, 104–5, 112, 140*

Schooling, *56, 93, 123, 140*

School intervention, *3, 5, 19, 39, 51–4, 56, 58–62, 65–7, 70–7, 80, 85, 90–1, 94–5, 101–3, 107, 109–11, 115–7, 119–20, 127, 138, 140*

School involvement, *120, 140*

School leaders, *56, 81, 96, 102, 140*

School newspaper, *87, 141*

School operations, *66, 77, 86, 107, 116, 141*

School personnel, *19, 55, 72, 105, 110, 124, 129, 141*

School policy, *3, 51–2, 54, 70, 76–7, 79, 83, 86–8, 90, 96, 105–7, 110, 115–7, 120, 126, 132, 141*

School professionals, *2, 27, 29, 70–1, 91, 95–6, 141*

School response, *37, 72, 141*

School rules, *49, 141*

School safe, *54, 141*

School safety, *54, 141*

School setting, *8, 13, 31, 42, 54, 57, 93, 111, 126, 141*

Schoolyard (see: Bully)

Scrutiny, *27–8, 67, 141*

Search, *79, 111–2, 141*

Self-esteem, *23, 30, 128, 141*

Self-injury, *69, 141*

Semi-naked images, *12, 141*

Sensible policy (see: Intervene - Intervention)

Sexting, *12, 129–30, 141*

Sexual orientation, *2, 141*

Share information, *17, 141*

Sharing comments, *111, 141*

Social, *2, 4, 7–14, 18, 22, 28, 30–1, 36, 54, 69–70, 72, 124–5, 128–31, 133–4, 139, 141*

Social changes, *30, 141*

Social concern, *22, 141*

Social cruelty, *11, 141*

Social experience, *7, 141*

Social happening, *28, 141*

Social media, *8, 36, 128, 130, 141*

Social problem, *7–8, 10, 12–4, 141*

Social settings, *2, 141*

Social trend, *4, 141*

Societal crisis (see: Bullying)

Society, *4, 8–13, 15, 17–8, 22, 30, 41, 51, 124, 129–30, 134, 141*

Stressors, *18, 141*

Shaming, *18, 50, 141*

Student, *2–3, 11–2, 18, 22–4, 29, 33–8, 41–6, 48–52, 55–6, 60, 65–7, 69–71, 73, 76–7, 79–80, 85–7, 89–91, 94–6, 101–2, 105, 108, 110–2, 116–7, 123, 125, 128, 131, 133, 137, 141–2*

Females, *12, 29, 141*

Right, *3, 34, 49–51, 55–6, 59–61, 63, 70, 73–7, 86–7, 89, 96, 102–3, 106–7, 111–2, 117, 126, 130–1, 137–8, 141*

Student activities, *60, 141*

Student behavior, *34, 70, 80, 112, 141*

Student behavior online, *70, 141*
Student behaviors, *91, 141*
Student being, *108, 141*
Student conduct, *3, 43, 141*
Student conduct online, *3, 43, 141*
Student expression, *50, 141*
Student expulsion, *49, 141*
Student harassment, *94, 141*
Student interactions, *36, 141*
Student journalists, *87, 141*
Student misconduct, *102, 141*
Student rights, *51, 73, 102, 111, 141*
Student speech, *87, 141*
Study, *12, 28–9, 33–5, 44, 46, 48–9, 71,*
    75, 80, 86, 90, 94–6, 115–6, 118, 123,
    131, 135, 141
Subside, *35, 141*
Substantial (see: Disrupt - Disruption)
Suicide, *8–9, 67, 69, 71, 108, 133, 135,*
    141
    Suicidal, *23, 69, 141*
        Suicidal feelings, *23, 141*
        Suicidal ideation, *69, 141*
        Suicidal inclinations, *23, 141*
Suing schools (see: School - Parent)
Susceptible, *16, 23, 67*
    Susceptible to commit suicide *67*
    Susceptible to depression *23*
    Susceptible to online bullies *16*
T
Tablet, *112, 141*
Target, *42, 141*
Targeted, *24, 141*
Technological, *10, 141*
Technologically, *9, 141*
Technology, *1–2, 9–10, 16–7, 23, 35–6,*
    42, 45, 56, 125, 127, 129, 141
Teenage, *8, 141*
Teenager, *8, 141*
Teens, *29, 108, 141*
Text, *2–3, 12, 22–3, 120, 141*
Threat, *2, 10, 24, 45–6, 80, 108, 124,*
    132, 141, 145
Tinker, *50–1, 111, 133, 141*
    Tinker standard, *51, 141*
Tormented, *42, 49, 134, 141*

Traditional, *8, 10, 23–4, 27–8, 33–5, 44,*
    48, 90, 96, 102–3, 110, 131, 139, 141
U
Unfair, *67, 142*
Unpredictable, *52, 73, 142*
Unproductive, *57, 142*
Unrealistic, *22, 142*
Unsystematic, *67, 142*
Unwise, *86, 120, 142*
Utility, *18, 142*
V
Vague, *51–2, 83, 90, 96, 116, 142*
Victim, *10, 24, 43, 91, 142*
Victimization, *15, 17, 22, 25, 54, 124,*
    133, 142
Victimize, *16, 142*
Victimized, *30, 34, 44, 108, 142*
Victims, *23–4, 29, 35, 37, 42, 44–5, 47,*
    66, 71, 108, 127–8, 142
Violated, *60, 65, 81, 87, 142*
Violates, *111, 142*
Violation, *50, 65, 73, 111, 138, 142*
Violence, *10, 54, 130, 142*
Virulent, *28, 46–7, 142*
Vulnerable, *16, 30, 37, 108, 142*
W
Warning, *49, 142*
Whole-school, *54, 142*
Women, *29, 45, 142*
Workplace, *7, 129–30, 142*
Worldwide, *48, 142*
Y
Young, *11, 15–6, 18, 21, 24, 29–30, 34,*
    37, 48, 54, 66, 69, 108, 124, 126, 134,
    138, 140, 142
    Young adults, *15, 142*
    Younger children, *16, 142*
    Young people, *11, 16, 66, 142*
    Young students, *18, 142*
Young adolescents, *18, 142*
Youth, *8, 10, 12, 16–7, 46, 69, 72, 126–7,*
    129–30, 132, 134, 137, 142
Z
Zero-tolerance, *48, 67, 142*

ABOUT THE AUTHOR

BEN WOOD JOHNSON, Ph.D.

Ben W. Johnson is an author, educator, and philosopher. He is a retired police officer. As a 27-year veteran of law enforcement, Dr. Johnson is a Fort Leonard Wood police graduate from the International Criminal Investigative Training Assistance Program (ICITAP). He is also a graduate from the Diplomatic Security Service (Mobile Division).

Dr. Johnson is a retired diplomatic security officer, with expertise in close protection/presidential security, intelligence, counter ambush/terrorism, anti-riot, special weapons and tactics, and national security specialist. During his police career, Dr. Johnson held various police assignments, including patrol, anti-riot, investigation, border control, special unit response team, counter ambush, team commander, administration, scout lead driver (presidential motorcade), advanced team, counterintelligence, translator, logistics, and training.

Dr. Johnson has taught criminal justice subjects at police academies. He has taught special operations techniques to veteran police officers. Dr. Johnson is an adjunct faculty member in criminal justice at Penn State University, Harrisburg. He holds a doctorate in educational leadership and administration. His academic background includes education, law, political science, public administration, and criminal justice. His research interests include policing in America, race and crime, law, school leadership, administration, and foreign politics.

Dr. Johnson writes about legal theory, education, public policy, politics, race and crime, and ethics. He is fluent in French, Spanish, Portuguese, and Italian. He enjoys reading, poetry, painting, and music. You may contact Dr. Johnson by e-mail or via postal services. See other information below.

ALSO BY

Selected works by Dr. Ben Wood Johnson

- Racism: What is it?
- Sartrean Ethics: A Defense of Jean-Paul Sartre as a Moral Philosopher
- Jean-Paul Sartre and Morality: A Legacy Under Attack
- Sartre Lives On
- Forced Out of Vietnam: A Policy Analysis of the Fall of Saigon
- Natural Law: Morality and Obedience
- Cogito Ergo Philosophus
- Le Racisme et le Socialisme: La Discrimination Raciale dans un Milieu Capitaliste
- International Law: The Rise of Russia as a Global Threat
- Citizen Obedience: The Nature of Legal Obligation
- Jean-Jacques Rousseau: A Collection of Short Essays
- Être Noir : Quel Malheur !

- L'homme et le Racisme: Être Responsable de vos Actions et Omissions
- Pennsylvania Inspired Leadership: A Roadmap for American Educators
- Adult Education in America: A Policy Assessment of Adult Learning
- Striving to Survive: The Human Migration Story
- Postcolonial Africa: Three Comparative Essays about the African State
- Surviving the Coronavirus
- Go Back Where You Came From

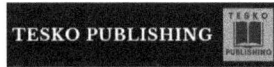

TESKO PUBLISHING

www.teskopublishing.com

www.ingramcontent.com/pod-product-compliance
Lightning Source LLC
Chambersburg PA
CBHW021334090426
42742CB00008B/603